BLOSSOMS OF BLISS

BLOSSOMS OF BLISS

*How to Live Today for a Better
Tomorrow*

Moesha Dharma
and
Digish Patel

The Book Guild Ltd
Sussex, England

First published in Great Britain in 2003 by
The Book Guild Ltd
25 High Street
Lewes, East Sussex
BN7 2LU

Typesetting in Times by
Acorn Bookwork, Salisbury, Wiltshire

Printed in Great Britain by
Bookcraft (Bath) Ltd

A catalogue record for this book is available from
The British Library.

ISBN 1 85776 765 9

CONTENTS

INTRODUCTION

'You yourself are three persons, not one: the one you think you are, the one others think you are, and the one you really are. The one you really are is God. God is in you, with you, above you, around you, behind you. All of you are Divine in reality.'

Sathya Sai Baba

Life is hard. Daily we strive to gain success, wealth, recognition and emotional stability. Yet in those rare moments that we stop and contemplate, it is often difficult to find any real meaning in our life at all.

Yet life does not have to be a constant battle. In the Vedas it says, '*Easwara Sarva Bhutanam*', which translates as 'God is indweller of all beings'. Quite simply, this means that we are all Divine, each one of us a spiritual being in a physical body.

Why do we constantly hanker for money, power and status? We do it to try to overcome our deep-seated *fear*, a fear that has arisen out of a lack of *truth* in our lives. Our true spirit, our true identity – which is separate from our body, mind and senses – is *fearless* yet very humble. If we discard our ego, and with it our constant quest for superiority, then we discover our true power – LOVE.

The mind creates an illusion (*Maya*), which it thinks is reality, based on its own thoughts, desires and beliefs. We cannot see the reality, which is God, because our mind is clouded by lifetimes of ignorance.

1

As E.B. Fanibunda writes in *Vision of the Divine*, 'By the evidence supplied to us by the modern physical sciences we may conclude that the ultimate nature of all matter, whether solid, liquid or gaseous, is primordial energy in a state of movement. In other words, this physical universe is constantly in a state of change and not at all stable. Its apparent reality and stability is a delusion, a hoax perpetrated on our minds by our senses.'

The root of all suffering in the world today is our false belief that we are only the body, mind and senses and that the Divine is a separate entity who can be conveniently forgotten whenever desired.

A person searches, either consciously or subconsciously, for two things in life. These are freedom from pain, suffering and want, and permanent Bliss.

Yet Bliss (*Ananda*) is the very nature of our true self and it is our inner self that is the source of the Bliss. Happiness cannot be found in lottery wins, fast cars, diamonds or big houses. If we wish to find true happiness we must look within.

People may try everything to obtain this Bliss in their lives. Self-help books, cassettes and seminars abound, but few of them make any lasting impression. To quote one man who we met at a 'Change your Life' seminar: 'I've been to all these workshops and I *still* get depressed on a Sunday night when I do the washing up.'

Sathya Sai Baba gave this book, its contents and its title, to Digish in a dream on 1st June 2001. In the following chapters we describe the six Human Values that every one of us needs to restore to our lives if we are to find a way out of the incredible human suffering that we see around us every day.

These Human Values are preached by many religions

and are the basic values that we should uphold in order that we may be worthy of being called a human. They all interrelate, and help us to integrate our spiritual and worldly knowledge, leading to a more balanced way of life.

The Human Values are like a seed that is planted and then germinates, grows and eventually bears fruit. We shouldn't worry if we cannot implement all the changes that we want or need overnight. Small changes add up, and if we *all* make a few changes to our lives, then the world will become a better place.

Once we start to transform ourselves, life will get better and better. Imagine being able to wake up happy every single day! We never know whether today is our last on this earth and so we should make it a good day and love each day that we are given, no matter how exciting or mundane it may be.

'So many people enquire into the secret behind my smiling, happy face that when, inspired by Sathya Sai Baba, we were given the opportunity to write this book, I was glad of the chance to share some of my joy with others.

'It is a sad fact that most of us have forgotten how to live. Life has so many gifts to offer us if only we give it the opportunity to do so. Modern living has reduced us to a sub-human existence, yet by returning to the Human Values that are our innate nature, ordinary life can be transformed into a wondrous adventure.' D.P.

You don't have to believe in Sai Baba, God, yourself or anything, but if you slowly introduce the Human Values of Truth, Love, Peace, Right-conduct, Non-violence and Selfless service into your life, then you will become BLOSSOMS OF BLISS.

SATHYA SAI BABA

'Do not seek to measure Me or evaluate Me. I am beyond your understanding.'

Sathya Sai Speaks Vol. 3

Born to humble parents in a tiny Indian village over seventy years ago, today Sai Baba is considered by over thirty million people worldwide to be an *Avatar* – that is, a great spiritual teacher and an incarnation of God, equal to Rama, Krishna, Buddha or Jesus Christ.

Baba has declared that he has come 'in order to achieve the supreme task of uniting as one family the whole of mankind through the bond of brotherhood, of affirming and illuminating the divine reality of each human which is the basis upon which the entire cosmos rests, and of instructing all people to recognise the common divine heritage that binds human to human, so that each one can rise into the divinity which is the supreme goal of human endeavour.' To put this more simply, we are all One and we are all Divine. To realise this is to gain liberation.

Sai Baba does not preach a new religion, but rather maintains that all religions are valid so long as they teach love and service to fellow man. He often uses the scriptures to illustrate his teachings, explaining how they have been distorted or misinterpreted.

The Early Life of Sathya Sai Baba

Sathya Sai Baba (Sathya means 'Truth', Sai Baba means 'Divine Mother and Father') was born at 9.06 a.m. on 23rd November 1926 and named Ratnakaran Sathyanarayana Raju. His proud parents, Sri Venkappa Raju and his wife, Srimati Eswaramma, lived in a thatched hut in a tiny village called Puttaparthi, which lies in the Anantapur district of Andra Pradesh, Southern India.

Sathya was a loving, gentle and kind child who seemed to possess extraordinary intelligence. At the age of seven he was a genius at dance; at the age of ten he taught the *Vedas* to the village elders despite never having studied them himself.

Sathya is known to have performed many miracles from an early age. He could materialise fruit, sweets, pens and pencils. He had a favourite tamarind tree, which can still be seen today, on the banks of the Chitravati River. From this 'Wishfulfilling Tree' the young Sathya could pluck any fruits that his friends desired, even ones that were out of season.

Sathya's family ate meat but he loved animals and refused to eat them. He used to spend much of his time at a nearby Brahmin lady's house, where he could eat pure vegetarian food.

When Sathya attained high school age he was sent to stay with his elder brother's family in Urvakonda. They forced him to perform incredible chores but he never once complained. On 23rd May 1940 a scorpion bit Baba's toe and from that day onwards he started behaving very strangely.

His worried family took him to a witch doctor who shaved off all his hair, cut his scalp and poured irritants into the wounds. Sathya's eyes and head became very swollen but his behaviour was unchanged.

Eventually, Sathya's father became tired of his son's odd ways. One day, when he saw him materialising sweets and flowers, he started threatening him. Sathya's response was not what his father had anticipated, for on 20th October 1940, at the age of thirteen and a half, 'He cast aside the books He was carrying and called out, "I am no longer your Sathya, I am Sai ... I am going. I don't belong to you. *Maya* [illusion] has gone. My devotees are calling Me. I have My Work. I cannot stay any longer." '

Sathya Sai Baba returned to Puttaparthi, where increasing numbers of followers gathered as his fame grew.

Shirdi Sai Baba

When Sathya announced that he was Sai, he declared that he was an incarnation of the first Sai Baba, who had lived in Shirdi for most of his life.

Shirdi Baba is thought to have been born to a Hindu family in the state of Hyderabad in 1838, but was abandoned at birth. A Muslim couple found and adopted him.

In the 1870s, he appeared and settled in a Muslim mosque in Shirdi, near Bombay. He kept a fire burning constantly and was able to turn water into oil to keep his lamps lit at night.

Shirdi Baba used ash for miracles and for healing, and today Sathya Sai Baba materialises *vibuti* (sacred ash) for his devotees. It symbolises the life–death cycle in which everything is ultimately reduced to ash and so reminds people of how they should give up material attachments. In addition, it has powerful healing qualities.

Little attention was paid to Shirdi Baba during his lifetime, although people began to flock to Shirdi for healing during the last ten to eighteen years of his life. It was only after his death in 1918 that Shirdi Sai Baba was recognised as an *Avatar*.

Prashanti Nilayam – 'Abode of the Highest Peace'

Baba's first devotees from outside the village had to endure a trying journey via bullock cart and on foot, as Puttaparthi was almost completely isolated from the rest of India. A road was constructed as more followers arrived at Prashanti Nilayam, as Sai Baba's ever-expanding ashram became known, and now there is even a railway station and an airport.

Baba is five feet four inches tall and of very slender build. He has a large bush of black hair and wears an orange robe, except on special occasions such as his birthday and Christmas Day, when his robe is white. Baba eats very sparingly, avoids milk products or sweets, and has maintained a constant weight of one hundred and eight pounds for over sixty years. He never sleeps. Wherever he goes, an intense fragrance of jasmine follows him.

Sai Baba's Work

Although in the early days, Sai Baba's teachings were virtually unheard of outside India, in the last two decades the tempo of Baba's worldwide mission has increased dramatically. In 1991, the inauguration of the

Super Speciality Hospital eight kilometres from Prashanti Nilayam generated a great deal of international media interest in Baba and his work.

This hospital, the second largest in Asia, took less than twelve months from conception to completion. The architect was the London-based Professor Critchlow and Isaac Tigrett, of Hard Rock Café fame, was a major financial contributor. It offers free treatment to all and complex procedures such as heart bypasses, kidney transplants and brain surgery are performed with love by an international, highly qualified staff.

In January 2001, a second hospital was opened near Bangalore, operating under similar precepts. These establishments join the others that Baba has founded over the last thirty years, including a primary school, girls' and boys' colleges and an Institute of Higher Education (deemed University).

The education offered in these establishments is described as Education in Human Values. It is an integrated attempt to achieve perfection of body, mind and soul by following the principles of *sathya* (truth), *prema* (love), *shanti* (peace), *dharma* (right conduct) and *ahimsa* (non-violence). This EHV system is also used in other countries, such as Thailand.

One of Baba's recent projects is the Sathya Sai Drinking Water project, which has supplied seven hundred Anantapur villages with clean water.

Baba's followers include actors, pop stars, politicians and royalty, as well as ordinary people from all walks of life and countries of the world. It is estimated that one million people attended Baba's birthday celebrations in 1995.

The Three Incarnations of Sai

'I am Myself in the middle of a triple incarnation and even now only the seeds are sown. But divine seeds bear divine fruit and my plan is perfect, so don't doubt or fear ... Love and peace will return to the earth and cleanse the horrors and excesses of the dark ages which today pollute the very atmosphere.'

Sai Baba, from Lucas Ralli's Sai Messages for You and Me, *Vol. 1, 83–84.*

Some may wonder why Baba has chosen the present time to incarnate. He explains by saying, 'But man has been overcome by greed and desire, and has reached the very threshold of destroying the world. It is at this juncture that I incarnate in human form, not to save the world, for I could do that with a wave of My hand, but to show man the way to save his own world.'

Sai Baba has told his devotees that he has incarnated to make everyone realise that the same Divinity resides in everyone. People should respect, love and help each other irrespective of race, colour or religion, so that all work can become worship.

Baba has stated that he will live until the age of ninety-six. Prema Sai, the third incarnation of Sai Baba, will follow him. This third *Avatar* will promote the teaching that not only is God within everyone, everyone *is* God. This will be the supreme knowledge that will allow *everyone* to obtain *Moksha* (the state of absolute freedom, peace and bliss obtained through self-realisation).

Addresses of Sathya Sai Baba

The main ashram:

Prashanti Nilayam
Puttaparthi
Ananatapur District
ANDHRA PRADESH 515134
INDIA

Between February and May Sai Baba spends some time at the Brindavan ashram:

Brindavan
Kadugodi
(Bangalore District) 560067
INDIA

TRUTH (*SATHYA*)

'Truth resides in every human heart, and one has to search for it there, and be guided by truth as one sees it.'

M.K. Gandhi

Sathya is the Sanskrit word for truth. It is derived from *'sat'*, which means simply 'that which is'. The idea behind *sathya* is that truth alone exists; truth is not what holds good just at a certain time or place, but that which never changes. As Sai Baba says, 'Truth does not change or cease to be.' Evil, hatred, injustice, etc, exist only if we give them support; they have no existence of their own.

What is the place of truth in the modern world? Most of us can remember when, as children, our parents urged us always to tell the truth. If we ever 'forgot' their advice, it was difficult to ignore the little voice in our head telling us that we had done wrong.

Everyone knows when he or she is doing something that is not right. Truth and untruth cannot be confused. However, over the years, many of us become so accustomed to ignoring our 'inner voice' that the boundary between truth and untruth becomes blurred.

When we speak the truth we feel lighter. It is so much easier to speak the truth in our everyday lives, rather than complicating matters by lying to some people and telling the truth to others. How embarrassing when our lies are found out!

11

If children hear their parents lying then they will copy this behaviour as they grow up believing that it is normal. For example, someone might call us on the telephone, but we don't want to speak to that person. We ask our partner, or even our child, to lie by saying that we are out. Is this living the truth?

Sai Baba teaches that we should have 'truth in thought, word and deed'. Our thoughts, words and deeds are like seeds, which bear fruit in time. Hence, there will always be repercussions to truth or untruth in due course.

'One day, as I was coming out of the Underground station, I saw a toddler who didn't want to go the same way as his mother and brothers and sisters. He refused to go any further, and sat sobbing on the floor.

'This is like the Universe/Baba/God holding our hands and trying to take us to the next stage in our lives. Often we don't want to follow; we don't want this dynamic, thrilling life that is being offered, we want to stay in one place and sulk.

'I myself am guilty of this and am only just managing to kick the habit. I used to prefer staying in the situation I was in, even if I wasn't particularly happy in that situation, rather than moving on to a better way of life.' D.P.

We are not living in truth if we do not follow the direction the Universe is taking us. For some reason, we are always ashamed of the truth. Not only are we untrue to others, we are also untrue to ourselves, fighting that inner voice that would guide us if only we listened.

Imagine a world of truth, where all doctors, lawyers, accountants and even politicians were truthful! Truthful words radiate love and harmony rather than unhappiness and discord.

A liar is vexed by *fear* and where there is fear it is difficult to live in love and peace. Also, lies perpetuate themselves, as a liar will automatically assume that others are also lying, and behave accordingly. Take insurance claims as an example.

Let us assume that a number of people in any one year make false or exaggerated claims. The insurance company recoups any losses by increasing insurance premiums and by becoming stricter about what claims it will pay for. The following year, people will exaggerate their claims more, to recoup the larger premiums they have paid.

If this lack of truth continues, then we all suffer (except, perhaps, the insurance companies!).

Truth and Health

'When I was in my early twenties, I had to see my girlfriend secretly for a number of months. My parents did not approve of the relationship as my girlfriend was of a different colour, religion and culture. I was forced to lie about my whereabouts at the weekends and other times when I was seeing her, and became ill mentally, physically and emotionally as a result of having to live a lie. When I finally became truthful to my parents, they were able to accept the relationship, my health improved and my girlfriend is now my wife.' D.P.

This demonstrates that truth is the foundation of all good things (even marriage!). The fearless and unwavering pursuit of truth will lead to true health.

Truth and God

Sat is an important Sanskrit name of God. God is Truth and Truth is God; the two cannot be separated.

Where there is truth, there is also knowledge. Where there is no truth there can be no true knowledge. Therefore, the Sanskrit word *Chit*, meaning knowledge, is also associated with the name of God.

Where there is true knowledge (i.e. the realisation that we are all Divine), there is always Bliss (*Ananda*).

God is therefore *Sat – Chit – Ananda*, a combination of truth, knowledge and bliss.

'There are innumerable definitions of God ... but I worship God as Truth only.' M.K. GANDHI

How do we Realise Truth?

Life is one long search for truth. In our busy lives, we need to find a few minutes of silence each day in order to concentrate our mind and to help calm and quieten our soul so that we can hear our inner voice clearly.

Candlelight meditation can help with this: Sitting comfortably, take a lit candle and look into the flame. Imagine the light between your eyebrows. Move it from there to your eyes, to bless all that you see; to your ears, to bless all that you hear; to your mouth, to help you to speak only good words. Move the light to your throat, then to your heart. If you wish, imagine your favourite deity at the centre of the light. Expand the light down your arms and legs and then up from your legs into the lower abdomen and stomach area, then back to the heart. From the heart, expand the light to fill the whole room, house, town, country, world and universe. Sit quietly and feel this for a few moments.

Truth and love (our next chapter) are closely related. They are the only values worth living for. Without truth, there can be no love, as without truth it will be some lesser thing, such as infatuation or lust.

LOVE (*PREMA*)

'Start the day with LOVE
Fill the day with LOVE
Spend the day with LOVE
End the day with LOVE
That is the way to GOD'

SAI BABA

What is Love?

Love is a much used and abused word. Many a song, book and film have been written about love, 'whatever love means' – to coin a phrase made famous by Prince Charles.

'Love is patient, love is kind. It does not envy, it does not boast, it is not proud. It is not rude, it is not self-seeking, it is not easily angered, it keeps no record of wrongs. Love does not delight in evil but rejoices with the truth. It always protects, always trusts, always hopes, always preserves. Love never fails.' 1 CORINTHIANS 13: 4–8

Love is a tremendous energy, and something we all have within us. It is our innate nature to love and this love can be expressed in a multitude of ways, such as sincerity, tolerance, kindness and friendliness.

'SI VIS AMARI AMA' – *if you want to be loved, then love.*

If we hate someone, that hatred will come back and hit us, as we are all One. As Buddha said, 'When one person hates another, it is the hater who falls ill – physically, emotionally, spiritually. When he loves, it is he who becomes whole. Hatred kills. Love heals.'

Gandhi had a similar view: 'Hatred does not cease by hatred at any time, hatred ceases by love. This is an unalterable law.'

Mother Theresa of Calcutta spent the majority of her life loving those individuals society preferred to forget and explained, 'The worst disease today is not leprosy or tuberculosis, but rather the feeling of being unwanted, uncared for, deserted by everybody.'

She also declared, 'Everyone should seek the pleasure of loving others in their own hearts.'

Indeed, this is backed up by scientific fact. Newton's Third Law states, 'Every action has an equal but opposite reaction.' Thus, hatred directed towards an individual will invoke hatred back towards the hater, and vice versa.

The law of *karma*, an important concept of eastern religions, has a similar basis. This is the law that governs all action and its inevitable consequence: the law of cause and effect. The word '*karma*' is usually used to refer to those actions or consequences that must be borne as a result of other actions (good and bad) done in the past and especially in previous incarnations.

Children should be taught to love their peers, their teachers and the subjects they study at school. Many of us will know, from bitter experience, that when we

17

hate a school subject, it will hate us back, and this usually ends up with failed exams!

If we ever come across Hitler (wherever he has now incarnated), or other such perpetrators of evil, we should forgive and love them. Remember, by hating anyone, we hate *ourselves* also.

We must be given love ourselves, in order to give love to others; otherwise our love would eventually be exhausted. We need access to an infinite source in order to recharge ourselves. There are many different ways to recharge our 'love batteries' and different individuals will have their personal preferences. Beautiful scenery, walks in the countryside, religion, poetry and art: all these can give us the inspiration to love, and we should make a place for something beautiful and inspirational in our lives everyday. Even taking the dog for a walk in the park can be good for the soul.

It is also important for us to *love ourselves*. This can be the ultimate inspiration, yet 'self hatred' is rife and a cause of many of our personal problems. We deal with this in greater depth later in the chapter.

Yoga and Love

Many people who have suffered from 'self hatred' find that exercise helps them on their road to recovery. How can we love others if we are not able to love ourselves?

Exercise is a form of love, unless it is done to excess, when it is actually quite violent and can even harm the body. Yoga is a gentle form of exercise suitable for almost everybody. It can help to recharge our batteries so that we can carry on loving.

Yoga is often considered to be just another type of fitness fad, which will hopefully make us slimmer, healthier and more attractive. Most people do not realise that there is any more to yoga than the postures (*asanas*) they are taught in their classes. Yet yoga is so much more than this. It is an important spiritual discipline; a way of life, which aims to educate the body, mind and spirit so that we can ultimately achieve self-realisation and bliss. '*Yoga*' is a Sanskrit word meaning 'union', and the ultimate union is that of the individual soul with the Universal Soul i.e. God/ the Creator/ Sai Baba.

Over time, four different paths of yoga have developed. These all have total union, and hence self-realisation, as their goal. As we all have our own personalities and preferences, individuals may prefer one path to another. However, although an individual may choose a particular spiritual practice as their preferred path, it is important not to ignore the teachings of the others, otherwise imbalance may occur.

Karma Yoga – *The Active Path*

This is discussed more fully in the *Seva* chapter.

Karma yoga is selfless service, by which the mind can be purified. A karma yogi works hard, both physically and mentally. He or she aims to eliminate the ego together with its attachments, to serve humanity without seeking reward and to see the Divine that is within all things. This form of yoga suits people who prefer to be doing something active rather than the inactivity of prayers or meditation. Literally, their work is their worship. Mahatma Gandhi and Mother Theresa are famous *karma yogis*.

Jnana Yogi – *The Philosophical Path*

This is the thinking person's approach to spiritual evolution. The world is described as an illusion, and discrimination and dispassion are used to dispel this *maya* in order that one may become self-realised. This is the hardest of the four yogic paths.

Bhakti Yoga – *The Devotional Path*

Bhakti yoga appeals to those who are rather emotional by nature. We cannot, and should not, completely repress our emotions, so *bhakti yoga* teaches us how they can be refined into pure, divine love.

Many see prayers, chanting and the offering of flowers in churches, shrines and temples as the pointless acts of those with a weak personality. However, these acts channel emotional energy, which might otherwise have become anger, hatred or jealousy, into devotion. This, in turn, can help the devotee to radiate love wherever they go, spreading joy and love. Without love, action is worthless. Hence, 'Love All, Serve All', a quote from Sai Baba that is now the motto of the Hard Rock Café chain.

Raja Yoga – *The Meditative Path*

Hatha yoga, the 'yoga' we know in the West, is the physical branch of the meditative *Raja yoga*. It is a way of awakening and freeing the mental and psychic resources that lie latent within us, so that they may be directed towards contemplation of the Divine. The yoga postures are primarily intended to achieve complete physical, then emotional, relaxation.

The ancient yogis studied the many obstacles to

friend and I went to her aid, moving her suitcase, sitting her down and checking that she was okay, she became very frightened and nearly fainted. She subjected us to a barrage of questions, in an attempt to understand why we had acted as we had. She was very happy with the fact that we had helped her, but a little suspicious of our motives. She thanked us but said that she would get railway staff to help her to complete the rest of the journey with her suitcase.' D.P.

'If you want to attain me, cultivate love, give up hatred, envy, anger, cynicism, and falsehood.' Sai Baba

Love is so inspiring and exciting. Sometimes the 'thrill' of loving each day, and the chance it brings to spread this love, can make it difficult to sleep at night!

Love keeps us healthy and vibrant. When we live in love we can receive intuitive guidance (that inner voice that tells us what is true and good). Where there is anger, jealousy and turbulence, it is difficult to make pure and good decisions.

Great beings like Sai Baba are embodiments of love. They are like beacons of light, giving boundless energy to the great crowds they draw as they radiate love.

Religion and Love

'Every religion teaches you to love one another and you should remember that love is the greatest force in the universe. God is love in its highest form and man should strive to let that love manifest itself in his own life at all times.'

Sai Baba

The basis of all religions is love, yet religious dogma and man's interpretation of religion often succeeds in creating fear. Where there is fear, it is very difficult to love.

'My initial experiences of Hindu traditions, the Vedas, the Bible, my visits to church with my school and, later, visits to Sai Baba's ashram, were of fear. Everything seemed to point towards what we shouldn't do because it was *bad* – we shouldn't eat meat, drink alcohol or even go to the cinema too frequently. I wasn't a bad person just because I ate meat, and I didn't stop eating meat because I was fearful (although eating meat nowadays often comes with the real fear of catching one of a number of nasty diseases). Once I started loving animals and nature, I realised that killing animals for meat wasn't a nice thing to do. It was not LOVE.' D.P.

Love and Vegetarianism

'Even a hunter cannot kill a bird that flies to him for refuge.'

(Samurai saying)

The killing of animals for our consumption is not an act of love, nor does it follow the principle of non-violence (*Ahimsa*). Our body is like the temple of the soul and as such, should be treated with respect. If a simple vegetarian diet is eaten, this will:

— provide us with the essential nutrients and energy that we require
— maintain purity of mind and body
— help to safeguard our environment and the lives of our fellow creatures

A vegetarian eats no fish, flesh or foul. Vegetarians also avoid the by-products of slaughter, such as gelatine or animal rennet in cheese.

A vegan is a vegetarian who seeks to exclude, as far as possible and practical, all forms of exploitation of, and cruelty to, animals for food, clothing or any other purpose. In dietary terms, veganism refers to the practice of dispensing with *all* animal produce – including meat, fish, poultry, eggs, animal milks, honey and their derivatives.

Care should be taken to eat a wide variety of foods when following a vegan diet, in order to avoid deficiency of certain vitamins, such as Vitamin B12, and minerals.

With CJD featuring frequently in the news, and Foot and Mouth Disease dominating the headlines for most of 2001, The Vegetarian Society reported a massive increase in the number of people seeking advice and information from them in their quest to turn vegetarian. How much more evidence do we need to show us that we should not be eating meat? In the 21st century, is it necessary for us to kill millions of animals a year in order to satisfy our taste buds?

There has been public outcry recently as millions of farm animals were culled during the foot and mouth epidemic. These animals were killed for purely economic reasons, as foot and mouth disease is seldom fatal, and vaccination gives protection from infection. However, people conveniently forgot that most of these animals were actually destined for slaughter anyway. In fact, those animals killed on the farms were actually spared the cramped and distressing journey to the abattoir, with poor ventilation and no food or water, which they would otherwise have been subjected to.

Is This Love?

Public demand for cheaper and cheaper meat has forced farmers to cut their costs to a minimum. This means that animals destined for our plates must be 'fattened up' as quickly and cheaply as possible.

We therefore have battery farms for chickens where they are crammed into gloomy cages, debeaked so they cannot peck themselves or their neighbours when it all gets too much for them, fed with foodstuffs that make them grow at such an unnatural rate that their legs often cannot support their body weight and routinely given antibiotics and antimicrobials to stop them from dying because their living conditions are so poor.

The Soil Association has warned that 20% of non-organic chicken meat and 10% of non-organic eggs have been found to contain over fifty times the legal limit of drugs deemed too dangerous to use in human medicine.

The sight of a pig rooting around in the mud is a rare one these days, as most of the pigs we eat spend their short life in stinking concrete pens. Sows are often confined to metal stalls both when giving birth and afterwards, and their piglets are taken away at an unnaturally early age to have part of their tails and some of their teeth removed without anaesthetic. (Again, this is to stop the poor frustrated creatures damaging each other's bacon.)

Cows are also given growth promoters, routine antibiotics, and animal protein feed that they would not naturally eat – hence the spread of BSE. Dairy cows are subjected to endless pregnancies so that they maintain their milk yield. Again, this is achieved with the aid of various drugs, traces of which can be found in non-organically produced milk. Calves are removed from their mothers just four days after birth, and reared on a milk substitute, leaving the cow's milk for human consumption. Male calves are usually shot shortly after birth.

Vegetarianism and Health

The human digestive system functions best on a vegetarian diet. The human small intestine is between 5.5 and 7 metres long and is pocketed to extract the nutrition from a vegetarian diet, whereas a carnivore's intestine is much shorter and smooth.

Vegetarians have low cholesterol levels and fewer heart problems (unless they eat a diet rich in full-fat dairy products). They have a 40% lower incidence of cancer and are less likely to suffer from arthritis, obesity, diet-related diabetes, constipation, gallstones and many other diseases of modern society. This may be due partly to the larger amounts of fibre and antioxidants found in a vegetarian diet. Incorporating soya products into the diet has particular health benefits.

Research suggests that soya has anti-cancer properties, especially against breast and stomach cancer. It may also reduce hot flushes and post-menopausal symptoms such as osteoporosis. This is due to soya's rich phytoestrogen content. Drinking soya milk is an easy way to boost our daily soya intake. It contains a similar amount of protein and B vitamins, and more iron and fibre than cow's milk. It contains less calcium so it is best to choose a calcium-fortified milk.

Vegetarianism and the Environment

The dairy industry is responsible for the discharge of large amounts of pollution into the environment, as manure, methane gas and effluent from silage. Approximately one quarter of agricultural water pollution incidents recorded by the National Rivers Authority are related to dairy farming.

The annual loss of an area of tropical rainforest greater than the size of England is largely due to increasing demand for grazing land for food animals.

Vegetarianism and Politics

Some 60 million people in developing countries die annually from hunger and hunger-related diseases. Yet food in poorer countries is fed to animals so that meat can be sold to more prosperous countries. At the same time, people in the richer, Western countries spend obscene amounts of money every year on slimming products because their calorie intake is too high!

This earth, of which we are temporary custodians, only has a limited amount of agriculturally productive land. It makes no sense to produce meat when the same land could feed many more people if used to grow legumes or cereals.

Consider a field the size of two and a half football pitches i.e. five hectares (twelve and a half acres):

— If this land is used for beef production it will feed ONE person
— If it is used to grow maize for human consumption rather than for animal fodder it will feed FIVE people
— If it is used to grow wheat, TWELVE people will be fed
— If it is used to grow soya beans, THIRTY people will be fed

A cow has to eat so much grass to produce the equivalent of even a quarter-pounder burger because much of the energy contained in the grass will be 'wasted' as it is lost as heat during respiration; only 4% is converted to muscle (meat).

When legumes and grains are converted into meat by feeding them to animals, 90% of the protein, all of the fibre and all the carbohydrates are lost. This also means that meat is higher in price.

Some people find it difficult when they first change to a vegetarian diet. Don't worry – introduce changes gradually to let your body get used to them. It is important to experiment with what kinds of food suit your individual body best, and to try different recipes – don't stick to the same foods every day or rely totally on pre-cooked convenience foods.

Food is more important than we often think. After all, we are what we eat. Food affects our mind, our body and our actions; our thought, words and deeds. Hence, it affects our *karma*. The consumption of fish, flesh and foul is often thought to bring the mind down to the consciousness level of an animal, as this story illustrates.

'I had suffered for a number of months with the painful swelling and inflammation of my right big toe joint. I had consulted physiotherapists, doctors and alternative practitioners, but none could tell me exactly what the problem was, or how it could be cured. My foot would not fit into my shoe, I couldn't walk properly and the constant pain was beginning to get me down.

'In desperation, I consulted a Chinese doctor, who was qualified in both conventional medicine and acupuncture/Chinese medicine. She was very good, and after a few treatments I noticed some improvement to my toe. However, even with weekly acupuncture sessions and daily applications of a special oil I had been recommended, the joint was not getting completely better. I had discussed my lifestyle with the doctor at the start of my treatment, and she knew that I was a strict vegetarian, but after a few weeks she told me that, without a few changes in my diet, I would suffer with joint problems throughout my life.

I was told that I should add a small amount of oily fish to my diet, and also take cod-liver oil capsules, as this would help to lubricate and heal my joints. What to do? I knew that fish-oil was beneficial to the joints, and respected my doctor's knowledge and advice, but I had tears in my eyes as I forced myself to buy a few cans of tuna from the supermarket. This was against all I believed in, yet what use would I be to anyone if I became a cripple? I would just be a burden on my family and society.

'Within a day of starting my tuna and cod-liver oil, I noticed some (slight) improvement in my toe and my energy levels increased. What were more apparent though, were the bad dreams and violent, sexual feelings that I started to experience. I could see myself becoming more aggressive and less compassionate. My personality changed and I felt like my mind had been taken over. Particularly upsetting was a dream I had, where a shoal of tuna fish came swimming up to me. "We didn't think you'd let us down ..." they said sadly, before turning around and swimming off.

'Without a doubt, I knew that I had to stop the tuna and supplements, and soon I was back to my (much nicer!) former self. My toe is now completely cured, thanks to various veggie supplements and ayurvedic creams – and time, the best healer.' D.P.

Once we start to live in love, we start appreciating things that we have taken for granted previously – the trees changing through the seasons, the birds in the sky, the waves lapping on the beach. It is as if our eyes are suddenly opened again.

'I remember how Hare Krishna devotees used to annoy me whenever they tried to stop me in the street. What good could they possibly be doing with their funny haircuts and even funnier clothes? I used to think – get a job, get a life . . .

'Then recently I saw a group of them in Los Angeles. There they were, by Santa Monica beach, in the sunshine. They were having a great time, jumping for joy as they sang "Hare Krishna", praising their Creator for life. "Good on you", I thought to myself. How I had changed!

'They were demonstrating how we should love whatever we do, non-violently and with total joy and peace.' D.P.

Does Love Pay the Bills?

Well, maybe not directly, but surely if you reveal the potential love in your job, loving your colleagues, clients and work, this will make it easier to love everyone at home and therefore make it easier for you to love yourself. Consequently, if you value yourself and your health, then wealth will surely follow.

'It took many experiences, many of them unpleasant, to teach me that I should love my patients and see the Divine within all of them, at all times. Imagine a young, newly qualified dentist, who always ended up with jobs in run-down surgeries, working long hours to treat patients apparently intent on making the lives of all they met a misery, and with bosses who always made themselves scarce on payday. It was often hard to love under these circumstances.

'For example, there was the big, unfriendly drug dealer, who had an even bigger and even less friendly Rottweiler. The pair of them burst into my surgery all of a sudden one day and the man told me how he was going to set his dog onto me unless he was seen immediately. Apparently, the receptionist had told him that he couldn't have an appointment until that after-noon, and this wasn't good enough!

'I quickly jumped onto the worktop to escape the snapping jaws of the dog, which was making a grand effort to bite my ankles. Fortunately, I was eventually able to persuade the man that he should perhaps take his dog home, unless he wanted me to call the police.

'Then there was the elderly man who returned to have his denture adjusted. It was a metal denture, one with various metal clasps to fit around the teeth. As I invited the man into my surgery, I held out my hand by way of greeting. What I didn't expect was to have the offending denture pressed into my hand and my fingers closed tightly over it, resulting in the sharp metal clasps digging into my palm and even drawing blood. 'Now you know how it feels,' he growled. He was obviously more than a little upset by the sore mouth his denture had caused.

'A third incident was when a Rastafarian in his twenties attended an appointment with me. I was alone in the surgery, as I had asked my nurse to develop some X-rays for me. I invited the man to take a seat and sat down on my stool next to him. Suddenly he thrust his face right up against mine and started ranting on about Rasta supremacy.

"I've got me a knife, man, and I have to kill you," he informed me, in a matter of fact way. I knew that I had to stay calm so that he wouldn't flip, as it was obvious that he was mentally unstable. Then he said, "God has told me to kill you. The voices speak to me."

I thought that I should try to reason with him, so I told Mr. Rasta, "My God and your God are one and the same. Remember our brother Gandhi? We must live by his example of non-violence." As I spoke, I tried to concentrate on sending love energy into his heart chakra.

'This seemed to confuse my unfriendly visitor and he appeared unsure what to do next. Seizing my opportunity, I led him gently by the arm to the door. Suddenly he seemed as docile as a lamb, so I showed him the fire-exit door at the end of the corridor by my surgery and suggested that he might like to leave by that route. He did so without a second glance.

'After this third experience, I realised that I really had to work hard at loving all my patients, with the attendant need to crush my ego, otherwise Sai Baba/ God/ the Creator would keep sending similar incidents until I got it right.' D.P.

What are Chakras?

The word 'chakra' comes from the Sanskrit word for 'wheel' or 'disc' and has its origins within the ancient yoga systems of India. There are supposedly seven chakras located in the body from the base of the spine to the crown of the head, although they are located in the astral body (our Soul) rather than the physical body. The *chakras* represent the vibratory levels of the astral body, becoming subtler as they ascend. In the physical body, the seven *chakras* correspond to major nerve ganglia, endocrine glands and certain body processes such as breathing, digestion or procreation, although they are not made of any physical components themselves. Raising the vibration level of the chakras, through breathing exercises or meditation, for example, produces corresponding changes in the body, emotions, mind and consciousness.

The heart *chakra* is often used as a focal point for meditation in order to generate cosmic love.

Loving Ourselves

'Our greatest fear is not that we are inadequate. Our deepest fear is that we are powerful beyond measure. It is our light, not our darkness that most frightens us. We ask ourselves, "Who am I to be brilliant, talented and fabulous?" You are a child of God. Your playing small doesn't serve the world. There is nothing enlightened about shrinking so that people won't feel insecure around you. We were born to make manifest the glory of God that is within us. It's for everyone. And as we let our own light shine, we unconsciously give other people permission to do the same. As we are liberated from our own fear, our presence automatically liberates others.'

Marianne Williamson (used by Nelson Mandela in his presidential inaugural speech)

This quote highlights a problem that is on the increase these days – self-loathing/self-hatred/an inability to

34

love ourselves. How critically we judge ourselves, assuming (often incorrectly) that this is how others perceive us. We are too fat, too ugly, too lazy, too boring. If we don't have love and respect for ourselves, then how can we possibly love others? It is also more likely that others will hate us if we have negative feelings towards ourselves.

How often do we deprive ourselves of those things fundamental to our very existence – food, sleep, pure water, fresh air and exercise, whilst indulging in things that are often injurious to our health, such as overworking, smoking, alcohol and under or overeating? And then we wonder why we get ill!

'After reading the *Bhagavad-Gita* and the *Vedas* (ancient Hindu scriptures), I used to think, "Well, we are not the body but the Soul (*Atma*), so why bother looking after myself?" I used to overwork, under-exercise, and overeat in an attempt to fill the cold, emotional void I felt deep inside me – that void that disappears when we love others and ourselves. I learnt the hard way – I suffered with slow metabolism, weight gain, lethargy and was always getting ill.

'Remember – the body is the temple of the Soul. Give it the love and respect it deserves!' D.P.

Loving Ourselves Made Easy

Good food is gradually making a comeback in Britain but we still have some way to go before we reach the high standards expected in countries such as France. The French afford food the importance it deserves. They do not grab a soggy sandwich for their midday meal or, worse still, work straight through lunch, surviving on chocolate, cola and coffee until evening. Rather, they ensure that they take a couple of hours out in the middle of the day in order to eat a nutritious meal that will see them through to dinner without the need for snacking. Lunch for them is also a social thing – a chance to spread love!

We have seen how food affects our thoughts, words and deeds. As well as buying the best quality food that we can afford (vegetarian, of course!), the way the food is prepared and eaten is also important:

— The food should have been prepared and cooked with love, not with anger. (Choose restaurants carefully.)
— Give thanks to the Universe for the food before you eat it.
— Eat with good company. Eating with people who cause you stress will not be good for your digestion.
— Eat slowly, chewing your food properly. Don't shove food into yourself mindlessly, such as when driving or on the move.
— Try not to watch television or read when eating. Give the meal your full attention.
— Do not overeat or under-eat as a way of controlling or hating your body. As a guide to how much to eat at one mealtime, it is suggested that you fill half the stomach with food, one quarter with liquid, and leave the rest empty.

It is important that we include plenty of high-quality water in our diet. Dehydration causes sluggishness, tiredness and is often confused with hunger. Tap water is better than nothing; filtered water is of a slightly improved quality, and mineral or distilled water is of optimal quality. Distilled water is the purest water available, with all chemicals and minerals removed. A minimum of two litres of water should be consumed daily, more in hot weather and when exercising.

As for drinking alcohol or smoking – remember how our body is a temple? We should try to keep the temple as pure as possible.

In addition, we should spend time in the fresh air and the sunlight (even in the winter!). Make the effort to go to beautiful places – parks, beaches, lakes, and mountains. Enjoy nature – see it, feel it, smell it, touch it.

Exercise is important, but so is rest and sleep. Babies sleep when they are tired, but as adults we have become used to overriding our need to sleep. We feel that it is a weakness of the body that should not be indulged when there are so many other things that need to be done in our busy lives.

Lastly, just as some people deprive themselves of food in order to feel that they have control, some of us go without things that we need to gain that 'holier than thou' feeling. It is obviously important to place a limit on our desires, but miserliness is not love!

Love at Home

'Love begins at home … But if you look in your homes, maybe you will see how hard it is to smile at each other. But that smile is the beginning of love.'

Mother Theresa

It is important that we learn to love and tolerate our own families before trying to love the rest of the world. This doesn't mean that you should spend all your time with relatives you don't see eye to eye with – just tolerate them. If there is love and harmony within a family, rather than discord, then that love will be contagious.

37

There are lots of simple ways to spread love within your home:

— Answer the telephone with love – smile rather than frown!
— Cook your family's meals with love; don't begrudge the fact that you have to spend time in the kitchen.
— Love your plants and they will thrive.
— Love the birds in your garden. They always appreciate food, especially in the winter. If you don't have a garden, then take some bread to feed the ducks in the park – a rewarding experience for all!

Too Easy ...

Let us consider the life of village women in rural Africa. They pound their cassava by hand, preparing it for eating. Smiling and happy, they sing together, thanking God for the harvest, blessing their food and generally having a good time.

Where 'modernisation' has struck, machines have taken over the women's job of cassava production. Although they are freed from their previous hard task, they do not sing or dance, and the children aren't so happy. What do they do with their spare time and energy? Nothing. The women are bored and frustrated.

Similarly, in villages where there is no well, villagers have to walk miles to fetch their water. However, in the process of fetching the water, they chat to friends on the way, meet people and also get exercise. It is a very social event. All this changes when water comes to the village.

No one is saying that modernisation is always a bad

thing, but we should ensure that it is actually improving people's lives rather than the contrary. Note how modern life gets easier by the year, yet less satisfying. Remember how, as a child, baking gingerbread men was so much more fun than buying them from the shop?

Central heating, ready meals, non-iron clothes, agencies who will arrange our social lives and even do our shopping for us. Does anyone ever stop and think that maybe the fun has been taken out of living, or ponder on the wisdom of working hard so that we can pay someone else to live our life for us? When we do get free time, we have so many things that we think we should be doing – we rarely use this time to enjoy the simple things in life or for mental and spiritual development. This leads us to wonder what is missing in our lives. We search and search, sometimes turning to drugs and alcohol in our desperation.

Many of us in the Western world are rather like animals in a zoo, which are fed, watered and mated without having to leave the comfort of their enclosure. Yet are the animals entirely happy?

We still have some animal instincts deep within our bodies, so it is no wonder that when we are robbed of meaningful activity and purpose we feel trapped and frustrated. This gives rise to a myriad of symptoms and illnesses.

We can use the time that technology has freed for us to do good, see good and hear good. We should relearn how to find joy in the simple gifts that the Universe bestows upon us: the joy of a friend's company, happy laughter, magnificent sunsets, and the smell of the earth after rain, even a trip round the shops!

Compassion

'First they came for the communists and I did not speak out – because I was not a communist.
Then they came for the Jews and I did not speak out – because I was not a Jew.
Then they came for trade unionists and I did not speak out – because I was not a trade unionist.
Then they came for the Catholics and I did not speak out – because I was not a Catholic.
Then they came for me and there was no one left to speak out for me.'

Pastor Niemoeller, political prisoner of the Nazis

The Chambers dictionary definition of 'compassion' is 'pity for another's suffering.'

Compassion springs from Love for All and is a non-violent, non-aggressive wish to free others from suffering, to give love unconditionally without expecting anything in return. If the compassion involves love offered with certain conditions or expectations attached, then this cannot be true compassion.

As we are all One, it is unjustifiable to sit back and ignore the suffering of others, whether in peacetime or at war. It could so easily be happening to YOU.

When offering compassionate love, we should try to ensure that we do not do so in a way that makes the sufferer feel that they are being pitied as this can cause them further loss of dignity. Take the concept of The Big Issue as an example.

As a vendor of Street News (the first homeless street paper, on sale in New York) explained, 'Normally when I'm standing on the street with my hand out, nobody wants to talk to me. They chuck me a coin and walk on. But with the paper people look me in the eye.

40

They're curious about me, what I'm doing, and why I'm doing it.'

By selling copies of *The Big Issue* on the streets of our towns and cities, the homeless person can once again feel that he is part of the human race and providing a service to his fellow men and women. Vendors are earning money through their own endeavours and not through the pity and indulgence of others. Some may gain the motivation and self-confidence to get back into mainstream work and off the streets. How simple it is to buy a copy of *The Big Issue* each week, knowing that a large proportion of the money you have paid for it will be going directly to someone who needs it.

'As I was walking down the High Street one sunny afternoon, the *Big Issue* vendor regaled me with his usual hopeful cry of, *"Big Issue*, madam?" I went over to him, stroked his dog, and reached for my purse.

"How are you?" he asked me, polite as always.

"I'm all right, thanks, how are you?" I replied.

"Not so good. I haven't sold any *Big Issues* today", he said gloomily. I pulled a sympathetic face.

"It is still £1 a copy, isn't it?"

"Or as much as you'd like to give", he ventured hopefully. I gave the despondent man an extra £1 coin, hoping that it might make some difference to his day, and continued with my shopping.

'An hour or so later, as I wearily pushed my supermarket trolley towards my car in the now nearly empty car-park, I saw a lone trolley in the bay adjacent to that in which I was parked. Some one hadn't bothered to return it to the trolley park, preferring to forfeit their £1 deposit in order to save their weary legs.

"Great! I've gained a pound!" I thought to myself as I wheeled both trolleys to join their companions. I suddenly realised with a jolt that I had just been repaid my £1 gift. Instant Karma!!' M.D.

Love for the Environment

Selfishness seems to have pervaded the current human population of our Earth. We behave as if there is no tomorrow, destroying the planet and its resources with no concerns for future generations. At this rate, there *will* be no tomorrow.

The ancient peoples of the world had great respect for Mother Nature. The Aboriginals believed that the Earth would offer whatever they needed but only if they treated it with respect. They ensured that they lived in harmony with nature. For example, an overnight camping ground would be returned to its original state before they moved on. The indigenous peoples of Africa, even today, would not dream of eating a fruit without pressing the seeds back into the ground so that future generations can be fed. If every one on this planet adopted the Western lifestyle, we would need *five* extra Earths to support us.

Our rubbish dumps are being filled with consumer items like hi-fis and videos that have a finite lifespan. Very little is repaired in these days of the 'disposable lifestyle'. If we don't have the latest model DVD player, TV, computer or mobile phone, society makes us feel inadequate and so our less up-to-date models are cast aside to make room for their more modern (but only for a short while) replacements.

As many of us rely more and more on 'ready meals', consider the impact of their containers on the environment. In a hundred years time, the plastic dish containing your microwaveable lasagne will not have degraded one tiny bit. We can try, where at all possible, to buy foods with the minimum of packaging; for example, by buying fruit from a market stall (in a paper bag) rather than from a supermarket where it will probably be shrink wrapped in a polystyrene tray.

Buying local goods rather than ones that have travelled across half the world helps to reduce the pollution from lorries and planes. We see flowers from Cornwall travel to Holland via Lincolnshire. These are packaged in Holland then flown to North England and then onward to New York. Is this really necessary?

We owe it to ourselves to drink the purest water possible but as you select your water, think of the fate of your plastic mineral water bottles. Few neighbourhoods have the facilities to recycle these, so glass bottles may be a better choice. Recycling should become a way of life for all of us, but even this uses up precious energy, so consider drinking filtered or distilled water.

These days there are very few parents who do not use disposable nappies. Again, consider their effect on the environment. The plastic within them does not rot and the large numbers of them being disposed of every day means that they take up a great deal of landfill space. Why not give terry nappies a try? – they are cheaper and these days there are even companies who will wash them for you.

Even if we don't religiously recycle our packaging or avoid processed food, there is no excuse for litter. Most litter is non-biodegradable, so will be around for hundreds of years. Even banana skins and paper cartons take months to degrade. Jars, bottles and cans can injure wild, or even pet, animals, and anyone who has been on a beach recently will know what a dumping ground our sea has become.

Carelessly discarded cigarette butts (what are you doing smoking them in the first place?) can cause fires, and the filters do not biodegrade easily. As for chewing gum – does it ever disappear? We should take some lessons from Singapore, where litterlouts face on-the-spot fines and the sale of chewing gum is banned.

When adults drop litter, children soon copy them. For them, it is one of their first examples of disrespect for our environment.

Petrol is a finite energy source and a major contributor to the pollution in our cities. Yet some people seem to have forgotten what their feet are for. Think next time you reach for the car keys – is your car journey really necessary or could you walk instead? Car share or cycling should be considered, or even, dare we suggest it, public transport!

Cycling or walking share the obvious advantage of improving our fitness and making us feel better. Does it make sense to take the car to the gym so that we can spend time on the running machine?

Keeping our Homes Healthy and Helping the Environment

Few of us realise that there are actually more pollutants inside the home than outside. According to some studies, air in the average home contains toxin levels up to seventy times greater than the outdoor air.

Where do these come from? Construction materials and furnishings are full of chemicals that release volatile organic compounds (VOCs) into the air. Natural materials such as wood, water based paints and untreated wool carpets with jute backing are to be preferred, but the type of wood is important. All wooden furniture and timber should come from sustainable sources. Mahogany should be avoided, to try to help conserve the rainforests.

Not everyone has control of the construction or contents of their home but we can all ensure that our homes are adequately ventilated by opening windows, and using natural air filters like spider plants to help absorb any chemicals that might be present.

Cotton is a good choice for natural bedding and clothing, but be aware that cotton production uses 25% of the world's pesticide output. Organically produced cotton is now available and is grown without the use of chemicals.

Household Chemicals

Many of the ingredients of our household cleaners sound like they should be in a laboratory rather than in the cupboard under the sink. There are many simple solutions to household problems. They do not come in pretty containers but they are very cheap! For example, vinegar cleans windows and washing soda unblocks drains. Most supermarkets now stock biodegradable, environmentally friendly alternatives to harsh washing powders, bleach and kitchen and bathroom cleaners. 'Ecoballs' wash clothes without the need for any detergent.

Energy efficiency

Domestic energy consumption is responsible for 25% of the UK's carbon dioxide emissions. Using loft insulation, fitting double glazing and using low-energy light bulbs will make a big difference to your household energy consumption. When choosing a new household appliance such as washing machine, freezer or dishwasher, try to pick the most energy efficient model available. Maybe you could consider installing solar panels to heat your hot water.

Household energy consumption, and hence carbon dioxide production, can also be easily reduced in the following ways:

— Turn lights off when leaving the room
— Turn down the central heating thermostat by a degree or two
— Put lids on cooking pots
— Only boil just as much water as you actually need in a kettle
— Switch televisions and videos off at the wall rather than leaving them on standby (when they are still using energy)

Organic Food

Organic foods are produced without chemical fertilisers or pesticides either on the crops themselves or on the land on which they are grown.

20% of all UK shoppers buy at least one organic product a week, but do we all know exactly why 'eating organic' is better for our bodies and the environment?

Why Organic is Better
1) Organic food is grown without the use of chemical pesticides, fungicides and herbicides that could harm the body. No one is sure of the exact cumulative/interactive effect of these toxins in the body. Pesticide residues in food have been linked with cancer and other health problems. Traces of antibiotics,

dioxin and DDT from intensely farmed food have been found in breast milk. These chemicals are neurotoxic and can damage a baby's delicate nervous system.

2) Fresh organic produce has been proven to contain more vitamins, minerals and enzymes than that farmed conventionally. Many organic fruits and vegetables also have a superior taste.

3) Buying organic is the only way to avoid eating genetically modified food. Even the food of organic animals (for those meat eaters amongst you) is GMO free.

4) Organic standards prioritise animal welfare. Animals have access to fields, shelter and daylight. Livestock is never given routine antibiotics (linked with antibiotic-resistant strains of disease in humans), or growth promoters, and is not fed on animal protein feeds. There has never been a reported case of BSE in British organic cattle.

5) Organic farmers are required to care for the countryside. This includes maintaining hedgerows, streams, planting trees, etc. Surveys show that there are more birds and butterflies on organic farms. (Those of us who were born in the 1970s and earlier will remember what butterflies look like. These days butterflies are increasingly rare.)

6) Organic farms generally employ more people and so contribute to the rural economy.

7) Intensive farming can seriously damage both farm workers' health (e.g. fertility problems and skin problems from exposure to chemicals) and the environment. Environmental damage includes soil erosion, the destruction of the natural habitats of various forms of wildlife and the pollution of our water by pesticides. The Government spends £121

million a year removing agricultural pesticides from our water so that it meets the standard required under EU law. As organic farming does not use synthetic pesticides, this reduces dependence on non-renewable resources.

The use of agro-chemicals to increase crop yields first became widespread after the Second World War, when governments needed a way to protect their people from the food shortages seen during wartime. Government subsidies encouraged the use of new chemical technology developed in the 1950s.

However, since the 1970s we have had huge surpluses of food (remember the lakes of milk and mountains of butter?) Yet still taxpayers' money is used to subsidise intensive farming. Organic farming receives no subsidies at present. Maybe this will change as the demand for organic food increases?

Genetically Modified Food

Food can now be modified to alter its properties or characteristics, for example, to make it more resistant to pests when growing. This is done by transferring genes between species, and may involve putting insect or fish genes into plants. No one knows the long-term implications of genetic modification, although there have already been some worrying findings. These include weeds becoming resistant to known weed-killers, and an increase in allergic reactions caused by foods.

GM foods were heralded as the way to end famine and starvation in underdeveloped countries, yet Steve Smith, director of Novartis (one of the largest biotech companies) is quoted as saying, 'If anyone tells you that GM is going to feed the world, tell them that it is not. To feed the world takes political and financial will – it is not about production and distribution.'

One Last Thought

HUMANS
ANIMALS
LAND
AIR

These are all constantly interacting, with the exchange of carbon and oxygen atoms. We are ALL ONE and abuse of the environment equates to SELF ABUSE. The human race cannot ignore the delicate balance of the planet without catastrophic results.

PEACE (*SHANTI*)

'There is nothing to be gained except awareness of what already is.
Simply be – *that is the state of bliss, of peace and truth and love.'*

Sai Baba (Thought for the Day 26/10/01)

We may have intellect; we may have wealth, but all this is worthless unless we have peace.

The best advice a parent can give to a child is this: When you grow up, do not worry about what you earn, what job you do or what you look like. The most valuable status to strive for is that of peace of mind, the ability to sleep soundly in your bed at night without mental turmoil.

We can travel far and wide searching for peace. Money cannot by it, just as money cannot buy love. Peace is always there within you; you just have to find it!

Consider the statement I WANT PEACE.
If we rid ourselves of ego (I);
If we rid ourselves of desires (WANT) – then we are left with PEACE!

Once we rid ourselves of anger, greed, lust, jealousy, attachment and other desires, we then achieve peace of mind.

50

'Only thoughts of God and intense love for Him bring peace. As worldly thoughts diminish, thoughts of God increase. As the desires are cut out one by one, the peace becomes stronger ... Swami cannot give peace of mind, one has to work for it.' SAI BABA

Once we lose our 'baggage' and our 'hang ups' we gain equanimity and henceforth, do not notice life's ups and downs. We are better able to handle both the good days and the bad days.

As our inner peace increases, the light of love within us will dispel our negative qualities and the perceived negative qualities of our companions and surroundings, just like the rays of the sun. We are able to expand our love to feel compassion. This love and peace will then spread from us as an individual, to our family, our community, and the nation and then throughout the world.

A Ceiling on Desires

In 1982, Sai Baba announced the following doctrine: 'Don't waste anything, particularly food, time, money, energy. The latter includes strong emotions like anger etc. Avoid unnecessary chatter and gossip. Avoid extremes. Where possible, use savings for the less fortunate.'

Food

'Annam Brahma – *food is God.*' Sai Baba

Gluttony is a desire that is extremely prevalent in the world today. No longer do we eat purely to assuage hunger and to fuel the body – nowadays we often eat

51

because it is time to eat or because something looks or tastes nice. Many of us have forgotten the true sensation of hunger and rarely is one's stomach completely empty.

John Kenneth Galbraith, a U.S. economist, has stated, 'More people in the world die from overeating than from starvation.' We need to remember that we are ALL ONE. If we in the West take more than our share of the world's resources and eat more than we need, this means that someone, somewhere will be going hungry.

Time

> *'Modern man thinks he loves something – time – when he does not do things quickly. Yet he does not know what to do with the time he gains –except kill it.'*
>
> *Erich Fromm, psychologist*

Science and technology have their place, but they can also move us away from our inner peace. Television is a very good example of this. As David Frost once said, 'Television is an invention that permits you to be entertained in your own living-room by people you wouldn't have in your home.'

How easy it is to switch the television on and then get sucked into its magical spell ... Before you realise, the whole evening has disappeared. Precious time has been lost forever!

There are educational and worthwhile programmes, and we do need to stay abreast of current affairs, but remember where the off button is!

News programmes always seem to be full of negativity. Advertisements raise our expectations of what we should be buying, or how we should be looking. For example, we are promised that 'this face cream will make your life so much better' and left feeling that maybe we aren't sexy enough without a particular brand of aftershave or perfume. Other media, such as newspapers and magazines, also set out to increase our desires, so disturbing our inner peace.

Money

> *'The love of money is the root of all evil.'*
>
> *Timothy, 6:10*

Money is entrusted to us by God and it is important that we keep our spending in check.

An increase in our desires needs a corresponding increase in our income, which may encourage us to resort to unfair means of getting money, such as fraud. Someone who takes more than one job to boost his or her income may be depriving someone else of the opportunity to work for a living.

'When I win the lottery ...' is a commonly heard expression. When we win money, when we are rich, then our lives will be perfect, we will be happy, we can do all those things that we always wanted to do – or so we think. We seem to have forgotten how to find joy in the present and how to enjoy the simple things in life; so intent are we on planning for that elusive day in the future.

If money brings joy and happiness, then why do so many of the world's rich end up as depressed drug addicts who exhibit anti-social behaviour and often have strong suicidal tendencies? It is because they do not have inner peace.

Things that we own usually give us joy for a brief initial period, then later, grief as they break down and need to be repaired or replaced. Our possessions need to be insured; we often have to pay hefty HP bills for them, and may even have them stolen (e.g. mobile phone, watch, car).

We may get attached to a certain possession, worry about it, or change the course of our day because of it. Take a large, prestigious and expensive car as an example. It cannot be parked in any old multi-storey car park, nor can it be left in places where it is likely to attract the wrong sort of attention.

Lightening our load by reducing our possessions may seem to be something that is undertaken on a physical rather than a spiritual level, but try it. You will probably find that it makes you feel good. As you remove unnecessary possessions from your life, your inner peace will increase.

'Whilst travelling around the world recently, for four months my only possessions were those I could carry with me. I noticed that when my belongings increased due to purchases made on the journey, how much of a nuisance it was to cart the extra luggage around, carrying the extra bags around streets and airports, packing and repacking them. My life was so much easier when I gave things away and reduced my luggage. I had fewer bags to watch over during my travels, fewer things to care for and I could use and enjoy to the full those things that I did have. I can honestly say that my inner peace during that trip was inversely proportional to the number of my possessions.' M.D.

The 'One In, One Out' Principle

'Just as one must not receive, so must one not possess anything which one does not really need. It

would be a breach of this principle to possess any unnecessary foodstuffs, clothing or furniture. For instance, one must not keep a chair if one can do without it. In observing this principle one is led to a progressive simplification of one's own life.'

M.K. Gandhi

We all need to replace household articles, clothes, and books etc on a fairly regular basis. If we get rid of old possessions equal in number to the new ones, then this will prevent our homes becoming full of things we no longer need. Charity shops will be overjoyed to have your cast offs, and there is nothing like knowing that you will have to give something away to make you consider whether you really need to buy something new!

Ego

'The ego is the enemy number one of spiritual progress ... It is egoism and its attendant evils that stalk the world today. Egoism breeds the scourges of greed and hate.'

Sai Baba

The mind, particularly the ego, is full of desires, and it is the ego that is one of the biggest hindrances to our 'peaceful' state.

Ego is the 'I' or 'self', that part of one that is conscious and thinks and has an image of oneself. It is the ego that gives us the desire to keep up with the neighbours, the ego that wants us to have the big house and big car so that people are impressed. Friends try to appeal to our ego when they tell us that 'if we valued

55

ourselves' we would get the latest camera, television or mobile phone.

Where does it all end? There will always be someone with a bigger house or car. Are they necessarily any happier?

The 'Monkey Mind'

Baba has likened the human mind to 'the monkey mind'. The monkey has the kind of mentality that can be used to the advantage of those who wish to catch them. When someone, such as a peasant, wants to trap a monkey, he uses a big pot with a narrow mouth. Inside the trap he puts some of the monkey's favourite food. The monkey finds the pot and puts its paw inside it to hold as much of the food as it can. Once it does so, it is unable to pull its paw from the small mouth of the pot. There is nothing holding the monkey apart from its greed. If only it lets the stuff in its paw go, then it will be free.

Energy

If we waste energy on developing our ego, this can lead to anger and unhappiness. Let us take criticism as an example.

If someone criticises us, we take it to heart and let the criticism hurt us. Our ego is damaged and we think, 'Why me? What have I done to deserve this?' Worse still, we may feel anger and violence towards the person who is criticising us.

Yet we can rise above criticism, by feeling the criticism but then letting it go without it hurting us. We shouldn't take criticism so personally; we may just have been in the wrong place at the wrong time.

Maybe someone was just having a bad day and we happened to get in their way! Do not indulge yourself in self-pity when this happens; maybe you were helping someone by allowing them to vent their spleen in your direction.

Take the criticism, but take the situation no further. Allow the anger to diffuse. If criticism and anger breed further criticism and anger, the whole situation can get out of hand.

'Assume silence when anger invades you, or remember the name of the Lord. Do not remind yourself of things that will further inflame your anger. That will do incalculable harm.' SAI BABA

Similarly, the judgement and criticism of others is a waste of energy and disturbs our inner peace. Also, it is probably none of our business anyway!

Silence

>*'The divine radio is always singing if we could only*
>*make ourselves ready to listen to it, but it is im-*
>*possible to listen without silence.'*
>
>   *M.K. Gandhi*

Much of the stress in our life comes not from external situations, but from our reactions to them. When we achieve inner peace we can 'stand back' from a situation rather than get mentally involved in it.

Silence helps us to find the peace within us. Many people find silence difficult and rather strange at first; some people actually fear silence. Maybe they are scared of what their inner voice is trying to tell them?

You can start in your quest for silence by finding some quiet time for yourself each day. Read if you want; paint, draw, sew or maybe even give yourself a manicure, but do it without the background noise of

57

television, radio or chatter. When you have become used to this, try to devote some time to complete silence of both mind and body. Maybe you could take the dog for a walk, find a quiet spot and sit in peace for a few minutes each day. However you prefer to do it, rest from activity totally so that you find internal silence. In this silence, you will hear the Truth.

'Remember when you see a beautiful sky, or scenery, all the internal chatter stops! For that moment we have peace – we must learn to increase this interval and we will get peace forever!' SAI BABA

Think of how much misery in the world would disappear if we all knew the virtue of silence. Unnecessary words often lead to misunderstandings and unhappiness. Not for nothing do we say, 'Least said, soonest mended.'

Before modern times, we were guaranteed at least six to eight hours of silence a day, but now life is a merry-go-round of artificial lighting, twenty-four hour shops and all-night television.

Mahatma Gandhi found silence both a physical and spiritual necessity. It was not unusual for him to spend a whole day or more in silence.

As you gradually manage to incorporate silence into your daily life, you will soon start to feel that you cannot do without it and that it reduces the stresses of modern living.

Prayer

> *'The man of prayer will be at peace with himself and with the whole world, and the man who goes about the affairs of the world without a prayerful heart will be miserable and will also make the world miserable.'*
>
> M.K. Gandhi

Prayer helps us to concentrate the mind and look within. It helps us to stop and reflect, and gives us the opportunity to think about others.

Many millions of people, both past and present, have found great joy and peace in prayer. In the morning it opens the day and focuses our mind on the hours ahead. In the evening, we can give thanks or apologies for the past day. By closing off the day properly, we are less likely to have dreams or nightmares.

Like the silence period, prayer is often difficult at first, but becomes easier with time. Prayers can take whatever form you wish. Through prayer you can get peace of mind, humility and patience. You can work on your faults and help the Creator/Universe/God to help you with them. You can pray for others.

'Some pray to a stone, some to a wooden cross, some pray only to the East or to different entities. However, all prayers allow us to quieten our inner self and, if we believe in God, to commune with Him.' D.P.

RIGHT CONDUCT (*DHARMA*)

'Just as it is the function of water to flow, for fire to burn and the wind to blow, each of us has a function to perform in relation to the universe and thus in relation to one another. It happens to be good not only for the individual, but for society and the planet.

Meditation, yoga, prayer, fasting, building energy by chanting and singing devotional songs, contemplation – all of these are ways of tuning into our personal dharma ... our special function that we are to carry out during each lifetime.'

Nazuna (Sai Diary of a Travelling Zen Lady)

What is *Dharma*?

Although there is no exact English translation of the Sanskrit '*dharma*', 'right conduct', 'right action' and 'righteousness' come closest to conveying the true meaning.

When love springs from the heart, becomes a pure idea and then manifests as action, this can be described as *dharma*.

How do we know whether something is *dharma* or not? Let Sai Baba explain:

'Let not that which you do harm or injure another ... If you injure another, you are injuring that same light that is yourself ... The test for dharmic action is stated very clearly in the Christian religion. That is: Do unto others as you would have them do unto you.'

If we try to see the Divine/God/Sai/the Creator in all and remember that we are all one, then this is an example of dharmic living. Imagine what a difference this would make to the world if every individual followed this principle!

We can use our will to help us to achieve righteousness both within our body, and with our body. For example, we can ensure that our eyes see only the good within things, our ears hear only good and our mouth speaks only sweet words. This also means no gossiping; using our hands to help society rather than to hurt people and our legs to take us to good places (rather than to kick people!).

We can avoid wasting food, water, fuel, time or energy. By avoiding the slaughter of animals for food, we leave them to work out their own karma. If our thoughts are positive, it is possible for us to avoid non-vegetarian food, smoking and drinking alcohol, but it is also important that we do not judge those who do indulge in these pursuits.

Ceiling on Desires

'I travel light; as light that is, as a man can travel who will still carry his body around because of its sentimental value.'

Christopher Fry

Another good example of dharmic living is when we place a ceiling on our desires. We spend our lives accumulating property, possessions, even children. We

61

should really think very carefully about whether we need something, rather than just acquiring it because we think it is what people expect of us.

Do we need a new car?

Do we need a child, or another child? There are so many people already on this planet who need our love and care.

Do we need that attractively packaged but empty-of-nutrition soft drink? If we are thirsty, why don't we drink water? There is a whole generation of children who are literally dissolving their teeth away because they refuse to drink anything unless it's brown and fizzy.

If we have something in our home that we haven't used for twelve months or more, then we should get rid of it. Why not sell it or give it to charity? It is only FEAR that makes us hang on to things that we no longer use – 'What if I need it one day?' we cry.

By clinging to our old things and ways, we are missing out on the chance for the Universe to provide us with those things we really need.

There is nothing small or weak about refusing to 'keep up with the Joneses'. It takes a much stronger character to be able to say 'no' to something that is unnecessary, and any money saved can go towards doing good within the family, the community, country or even the world.

'When there is righteousness in the heart there is beauty in character, there is harmony in the house. When there is harmony in the house, there is order in the nation. When there is order in the nation, there is peace in the world.' SAI BABA

All this is obviously going to be a little difficult at first, as old, unwanted habits are cast off. After a while, the habit of 'placing a ceiling on desires' can actually become rather fun as we realise how, in this life, we burden ourselves with things that we don't need and often don't really want.

As we make gradual steps towards a more dharmic lifestyle, the Universe will give us gifts, both material and spiritual, the nature and extent of which we cannot even begin to imagine.

Finding our *Dharma*

'Dharma *does not depend on an individual. It doesn't depend on a period of time or a particular destination.* Dharma *depends only on truth. That is why it has been said that there is no* dharma *other than truth. To conduct oneself in a manner which on the spur of the moment comes to one's mind and to think that that is* dharma *is very foolish. To think that to conduct oneself in accordance with one's own ideas is practice of* dharma *is very foolish. To be able to develop equal mindedness and to be able to develop equanimity* are *the correct aspects of* dharma *and for this one must have an unwavering mind and thought.'*

*Sai Baba (*Summer Showers in Brindavan*, 1974)*

When starting to practise *dharma* in our everyday lives, it is initially necessary to question every decision that we make. We must consciously ask our heart, 'Is this right?' It can be very tiring at first, as old ideas have to be given up. Gradually, our 'duty' in this life will unfold. What has each one of us as an individual got to offer this Universe?

According to Hinduism, we are all incarnate of the Divine, with love to offer and talents to express in

63

order to help Mankind. It doesn't matter what our particular talents are; it may be that we are good at 'pulling teeth' at Dental Camps, or washing the dishes at a Hospice. We will know when we are truly following our *dharma* because we will feel happy, healthy and satisfied and the time will fly by.

Sai Baba often gives his devotees a watch when they ask for help with their *dharma*. Every time they look at their watch, they are reminded how they should be behaving.

Words – should never be hurtful, should avoid gossip and lies
Action – is it worthwhile and good or is it ego-orientated? Will it cause harm to others?
Thoughts – are they sympathetic, caring, understanding and always positive?
Conduct – humble and righteous
Heart – it is *dharma* only if it has truly come from the heart

In short, *dharma* is harmony in thought, word and deed. It is when our head, heart and hands are in confluence.

NON-VIOLENCE (*AHIMSA*)

'Policies may and do change. Non-violence is an unchangeable creed. It has to be pursued in face of violence raging around you.'

M.K. Gandhi

Although the English translation of '*ahimsa*' is 'non-violence', the Sanskrit word has no such negative connotation. '*Ahimsa*' implies that when all violence subsides in the human heart, LOVE is all that remains. It is always there, and just needs to be revealed.

What exactly is *Ahimsa*?

'You consider ahimsa *as merely not hurting others. This is not the whole truth. Speaking too much, working too much, harping on the mistakes of others are all acts of violence (*Himsa*) and should be avoided. These result in the wasting of energy, which causes harm to oneself. You must observe restraints in eating, talking, sleeping, working and all actions in daily life.'*

Sai Baba, Sanathana Sarathi, July 1995

All life is one. Once we realise this, we must affirm that oneness by being kind, compassionate and respectful to all living beings.

65

As well as avoiding the more obvious actions that cause distress or pain to any living being, we must in addition watch our thoughts. If we think ill of someone or wish harm on him or her, this is violence.

Words, whether spoken or written, can do great damage to a person and the hurt they cause can last a long time. Sometimes it is very easy to overreact to a situation. Perhaps someone says something that offends us and we give a hurtful reply without thinking. We should try to love all and if we feel that we cannot handle a situation in the correct manner, we should try to dissociate ourselves and rise above it until we have calmed down.

Ahimsa also means not harming the environment, or ourselves or condoning another person who is acting in a violent manner.

We can no longer treat our planet as if it were a disposable commodity. For example, if we pollute the world's water, it affects us directly as our physical bodies contain a large percentage of water and we rely on clean water to survive.

Visitors to Sai Baba's ashram in India realise just how wasteful Western-style bathing can be. In the ashram it is possible to have an adequate wash with little more than a bucketful of water – compare this to the amount of water used by long showers and full baths. It is not necessary to renounce washing, but steps such as having a water meter fitted can be a good incentive to try to save water.

To practice *ahimsa* we must be constantly vigilant over every aspect of our life. Some believe that when we upset the delicate balance of the Universe, natural disasters such as earthquakes, floods and droughts are the result. We have scientific explanation for this in the form of Newton's Third Law, which states that 'for

66

every action there is an equal and opposite reaction'.

Vegetarianism is discussed more fully in 'LOVE'. There is absolutely no need for us to harm our animal brothers and sisters by killing them for food, or for any other reason. Consider the taking of an animal's life purely for fun, such as in bullfighting. Few would disagree that this is totally barbaric. Similarly, killing a wasp or a fly just because it is annoying is most definitely NOT *ahimsa*.

There are many examples of man's cruelty to animals that often go unnoticed by the majority of us. The live export of animals continues and it isn't solely confined to cows, pigs and sheep. Nearly 100,000 horses a year face the horrific journey, up to five days long, from Poland to Italy, where they are slaughtered by having their throats cut.

What message are we giving to younger generations about compassion and non-violence? If children grow up thinking that it is acceptable to hurt and kill animals, they are more likely to be violent in the future. Serial killers on death row in America share cruelty to animals as a common trait.

As the civil rights activist Dick Gregory wrote, 'Animals and humans suffer and die alike. Violence causes the same pain, the same spilling of blood, the same stench of death, the same arrogant, cruel and brutal taking of life.'

Overeating is violence to our body, as we have to process the extra food and then carry it around as stored adipose tissue. It is also a waste of food, which could have gone to feed someone who actually needed it.

Too much sleep and talking too much are also harmful and so should be avoided. The time wasted pursuing these to excess could be put to better use. Moderation is the key!

In native African and Fijian villages, as in other places where traditional values still prevail, the concept of 'hurry' is totally alien to those who live there. They see 'hurry' as an expression of anger. If we have no time for another person, or are constantly thinking of our next task and ignoring the present, it must be due to anger or hatred, surely. To live for the moment, to accept what the Universe has provided us with at that one time, and to love the moment – that is non-violence. Maybe we could learn a lesson from this as we hurry through our busy lives, constantly trying to juggle career, family and friends.

Although we often do not realise as much, by driving fast we are showing disregard for human life. Accidents do happen, but we can try to minimise the injuries and damage that they cause by observing the rules of the road and speed limits.

Similarly, we should pay regard to how we act if someone upsets us with their driving. Are we demonstrating love if we react with anger? It is just our ego that becomes offended. We should try to dissociate ourselves from the situation and let it pass without acting violently.

Arcade and computer games are very common and popular but do we really want our children growing up to think that driving fast or gun warfare is the way to behave? Individuals who spend a lot of their time playing these games often find that the distinction between make believe and reality becomes blurred.

Overworking – a Salutory Tale

Overworking is harmful to ourselves and often also to those around us. There are many different reasons why a person overworks – they may be doing it for greed, to prove themselves, because the rest of their life is empty, or maybe they hide in their work because they don't want to face up to reality.

'In 1998 my wife and I started our own business, an NHS dental surgery. We had thought about it for some time, looking at various premises, before finally committing ourselves to part of a brand-new building. We felt that opening our own surgery was the right thing to do at that time; it was a natural career progression and we were looking forward to being freed from the confines of working for other people. As we set about equipping the place and getting everything prepared, it was good fun, and yet rather daunting and frightening.

'We were not afraid of hard work and once the doors of our surgery were opened, it was an instant success. Everybody expects to have to work hard at a business initially, but I carried on working every hour I could long after I could have started to cut down a little. The surgery became my life. It became my excuse for avoiding anything I didn't want to face. Not only was I hiding from myself, (I felt that I had an excuse for neglecting my health and fitness as I was too busy working), but also from other people (what did they know about dental surgeries? Didn't they realise that I was too busy to spend time with them?).

'I was soon drawn into a vicious cycle. As I earned more money, our expenses increased as we felt that we deserved a better quality of life, and our taxes also increased. I then had to work even harder to earn more money to pay our expenses and taxes, and so it went on. I was working over seventy hours a week, sometimes fourteen hours a day with no break.

'With all this overwork, I sometimes felt angry and

resentful, but I always treated the patients with love. I loved the patients and put their needs to the fore to the extent that they ruled me. I would do anything for them, as I believed that that was how a business like ours should be run.

'I did not love myself, however. Ever since graduating as a dentist I had been binge eating to try to cope with periods of stress. Sometimes I would eat so much that I would feel sick. On a few occasions I did actually vomit. I was using the food to try to fill the ever-present void that I felt inside me, the void that the result of trying to cope with the violence, hatred and lies that I often experienced from patients, colleagues, bosses and staff. This binge eating had caused me to gain weight and certainly had an adverse effect on my health.

'After about twenty-four months I was tired, very tired. It wasn't so much fun any more. Yet I still loved and cared for my patients. At this point I experienced an extremely disturbing dream whilst spending a weekend in the Lake District.

'I was shown our lives ten years into the future. As the owners of multiple businesses, we were very successful and very rich. However, we had no life and no fun. One of us, I wasn't sure who it was, had a violent death on the steps of our home. We had lost contact with our friends and family, so the survivor had no support or comfort and no one to turn to.

'I then saw myself at Sai Baba's ashram. He was waiting for me at the gate. "I called you but you never came," he said. "You must do your work!"

'This dream made me look long and hard at my life. I had always known that one day I had to work in dental camps in poorer areas, and write, but I had got tired from all my overwork and all this seemed like too much effort. Surprising as it may seem, at that time I did nothing to change my life at all.

'A few months later, my left big toe suddenly swelled up overnight and became acutely painful. I could barely walk. I consulted doctors and had it X-rayed but no one was sure of the cause, or how to cure it. In desperation, we sat down and wrote a letter to Baba. In it we gave him an ultimatum. If we were to get rid of the surgery in order to change our life, do new work and have fun, then the surgery must sell immediately.

'The sale of the surgery was agreed within twenty-four hours of it going on the market!

'You see, for some people it is good to stay in one place; for others signs tell us that we must move on for various reasons. All I know for sure is that if you follow the signs, you'll have much more fun than if you don't!' D.P.

Other Examples of Man's Violence

War

Mahatma Gandhi devoted most of his life to proving that non-violence is the only way to resolve the problem of conflict permanently. We all know that violence perpetuates violence. To rely on violence to solve a problem will sow the seeds of bitterness and hostility that will ultimately cause the situation to deteriorate.

Non-violence is a subtle force but this does not diminish its efficacy; it actually makes it harder to oppose. Gandhi's 'passive resistance', which took various forms such as marches, fasts, boycotts and civil disobedience, was a truly potent force. Inside every one of us there is a tremendous power. When this power is revealed through self-discipline and adherence to the Truth, the individual is invincible.

Capital Punishment

It is a sad fact that the death penalty is very much alive in many countries of the world including the USA, which likes to think that it leads the world. How can a human being killing a fellow human be described as justice? To have the law on one's side does not make it any more excusable to take someone else's life.

Persecution and Torture

Remember, we are all one. The persecution of fellow man on the grounds of race, colour, politics or religion has no place in the twenty-first century. Ignorance or lack of understanding of another person's way of life breeds fear and intolerance. We may be narrow-minded and think that our ways are best. This leads to a desire to gain supremacy by violent means. All our fellow human beings are embodiments of God and we should strive to see the Divine within them, however hard this may seem.

'But I tell you who hear me: Love your enemies, do good to those who hate you, bless those who curse you, pray for those who ill-treat you. If someone strikes you on one cheek, turn to him the other also. If someone takes your cloak, do not stop him from taking your tunic. Give to everyone who asks you, and if anyone takes what belongs to you, do not demand it back. Do unto others as you would have them do to you.' Luke 6: 27–31

Abortion

> *'Fight abortion with adoption. Remember that each child is carved by God with His own loving hands and it is murder to destroy an unborn child.'*
>
> *Mother Theresa*

Figures obtained from the The National Office of Statistics show that in 2000, 23% of conceptions in England and Wales ended in legal abortion. Abortion seems to be considered by some as just another form of contraception. Many women in their early twenties opt for abortions for the sole reason that they want to concentrate on their career and having a baby would be inconvenient.

In the UK (apart from Northern Ireland) the law decrees that it is legal to end the life of a foetus up to the age of twenty-four weeks, if two doctors agree that to continue with the pregnancy would involve mental or physical risk to the mother or any existing children greater than if the pregnancy was terminated. The twenty-four week limit does not apply if the woman's life would be at risk if the pregnancy continued or if there is substantial risk that the child would be born seriously disabled.

Does this mean that an embryo or a foetus is an insentient, soul-less being up to a certain age when suddenly it develops feelings overnight?

Abortion is a very emotive and upsetting issue and there is no doubt that many of us would consider abortion justifiable under certain cirumstances such as cases of rape or if the child would be deformed.

No one should sit in judgement on a woman who feels that she needs an abortion and she should be entitled to all the support she needs. However, the

73

above statistics are a worrying reminder that we cannot become blasé about this matter and the fact remains that the deliberate termination of the life of an unborn child is not *ahimsa*.

What is particularly sad is the action of certain parents, particularly Indian and Chinese, who feel that they must abort a healthy baby girl solely because they want to try again for a 'superior' male child.

Lust

Jesus and Gandhi both taught that when we lust after someone or something in our heart, the damage is already done, that is, our thoughts are just as important as our actions.

When we are lusting after another person who is not our spouse or partner, all our five senses are aroused. It is difficult to control the senses, but by following the human values we can master them.

If this lust develops further, it is likely that lies and deception will be involved. The truth will be ignored. It may cause the breakdown of the original relationship or marriage, loss of self-respect, long-term psychological damage to any children involved, and maybe even an unwanted pregnancy.

Anger

'Whilst writing this chapter, Sai Baba, my inspiration, got a great deal of bad press. The majority of this had been initiated by those who professed to be on a spiritual path. Many people, including close friends, used it as an opportunity to attack our beliefs and us. My first impulse was to attack back, but to do this would be to act in anger.

'I had to understand that the first instinct of many, when faced with something inspiring, is to attack it as then there is no need for them to change themselves. Unfortunately, the opportunity for them to become a better person is then lost.

'We should indeed keep up to date with the news, but on no account should we believe everything that we are presented with. To do so would be to act with immaturity and lack of discipline. As Mother Theresa once said, "The press can build. The press can break." We must use our intelligence, common sense and heart to interpret the information we are given.' D.P.

Anger is an unnatural state and can make us mad, almost insane. Anger causes the body to become very tense and can cause illness and damage to our health. It is a violent, unpleasant emotion and should be kept in check wherever possible – counting slowly to ten really does help the anger to pass.

Vivisection

*'The greatness of a nation and its moral progress can be judged by the way its animals are treated ...
I hold that, the more helpless a creature, the more entitled it is to protection by man from the cruelty of man.'*

M.K. Gandhi

Animal experimentation may be to find cures for serious illnesses but many experiments are performed for trivial purposes such as the testing of household products.

In addition to causing pain and suffering, animal testing is actually scientifically unsatisfactory, particularly as the differences between humans and animals can give misleading results:

— Findings from animal models cannot be reliably extrapolated to humans.
— Inter-species extrapolation produces data from animal studies that is misleading to researchers and results in harm to patients.
— Animal experimentation diverts funds from more useful science-based research.

Causing suffering to animals in experiments is violence and is unacceptable in civilised society, particularly as there are alternative methods that can be used for research, such as computer programs, molecular research and the use of human-cell cultures.

Non-violence and Truth

Non-violence is the greatest expression of truth and indeed, *ahimsa* is the way to Truth. By following the pathway of non-violence to truth, we can achieve love.

'*Ahimsa* and truth are so intertwined that it is practically impossible to disentangle and separate them. They are like the two sides of a coin, or rather a smooth unstamped metallic disc. Who can say which is the obverse and which the reverse? Nevertheless, *ahimsa* is the means; truth is the end.' M.K. GANDHI

To follow the path of non-violence it is necessary to change our mental attitude. Only those who are ready to sacrifice their desires will be able to follow this route. We should strive to achieve purity of thought, word and deed; we should serve even our enemies with love; we should overwhelm the bad and the jealous by our goodness.

Humility is the characteristic of those who wish to assume the mantle of non-violence. It is relatively easy for a strong person to become non-violent, but a weak and cowardly person will find it impossible. Non-violence means the capacity to love those who hate you, and to show patience and understanding in the face of all opposition. It is the most difficult discipline one can learn in life.

The *Bhagavad-Gita* says, 'If you want to see the brave, look at those who forgive. If you want to see the heroic, look at those who can love in return for hatred.'

SELFLESS SERVICE (*SEVA*)

'When a person serves society sincerely and is no longer self-centred, the ego in him vanishes ... And exit of ego from a person's heart makes room for God to enter it.'

Sai Baba

Man's ultimate aim in life is self-realisation, the realisation that we are all Divine and embodiments of God. When we have achieved this we will be freed from *samsara*, the endless cycle of rebirth and death. Service to fellow man is an important part of our journey to self-realisation as the only way to find God is to see him within all humanity.

Through selfless service done with love, we can expand the heart, purify the mind and break down the barriers that stand in the way of unity and the oneness of all existence.

The human body is meant solely for service, never for indulgence. Service will bring happiness, not only for us but also for the entire world, whereas indulgence will always lead to unhappiness.

What Can We Do As *Seva*?

'We all do some kind of work, it makes no difference what we are doing. What you are doing, I

78

cannot do and what I am doing, you cannot do. But all of us are doing what God has given us to do.'

Mother Theresa

We are all constantly engaged in service of some kind. It may be in the office at work, or it may be doing the housework at home. If it is done with love and lack of self-interest then it is *seva*. Even opening a shop or business is *seva* if it is done with Truth, Love, Peace, Non-violence and Righteousness.

Our acts of *seva* do not have to be big or complicated. *Seva* can be as simple as smiling at someone. Think how easy it is to smile, yet to someone who is feeling a little down, a smile can really change their day and raise their spirits.

As Mother Theresa said, 'When you smile at each other, where is the need for words? I have found that I can go anywhere and be with people even though I cannot speak or understand their language.'

It is quite easy to do *seva* at home, by doing everyday tasks like cooking and cleaning with love. We may have opportunities for *seva* at work if we work in a hospital, surgery or shop, for example. Remember, it can still be *seva* even though we are being paid, as long as we are doing the job selflessly and with love rather than begrudgingly.

Blood donation is an excellent opportunity to give service. Baba calls blood 'liquid love'. At the present time, the only way to replace blood lost by an individual is to use someone else's blood and so blood donation literally saves lives.

Giving blood is virtually painless, only takes a few minutes and you get a free drink and biscuit afterwards! Mobile blood donation units stop at most towns and cities on a regular basis.

Most people equate *seva* with voluntary work and there are indeed endless opportunities for volunteers who have a little spare time to help others. These range from work in a charity shop, to feeding the homeless in soup kitchens or delivering library books or groceries to the elderly or housebound.

It is very humbling to see the way some people with disabilities work tirelessly doing voluntary work, when many other able-bodied individuals are just too lazy or unmotivated to do anything to help others.

When we are engaged in selfless service, whether paid or unpaid, we find that it is not only enjoyable and fulfilling, it is *divine*. When we serve others, we get an opportunity to both *give* and *receive* love and this in itself is very healing. Sometimes it almost feels as if we are being selfish as we get so much in return for our *seva*. Also, when we are busy helping others, we forget about any suffering of our own.

Selfless service unites all the human values of Love, Truth, Peace, Right-action and Non-violence, and puts them into action. As we have said before, it doesn't have to be million-dollar service to humanity, such as building hospitals or schools. It can be *seva* on a small scale (picking up litter if you see it as you go about your daily business, taking in a parcel for a neighbour, helping an elderly person across the road, for example) or even *seva* to ourself.

It is actually service to look after our body and our health so that we do not burden our family or the state by suffering with avoidable health problems. An action so simple as brushing our teeth can have far reaching health benefits – if we keep our teeth healthy we will be able to chew our food properly, so digesting food better and so contributing to our good health.

Tasks we might have previously thought tiresome

can actually make life more fun if they are done as selfless service, for example, washing and caring for the car, ironing, buying flowers for a loved one. If we see the good in all these chores, if we work to help others and in turn ourselves, then we grow in Love and eventually *become* Love.

As we enjoy nature, we can see how it serves – trees give us fruit to eat, clouds give rain so that we have water to drink and to help crops to grow, the sun gives light so that all living things thrive and cows give us milk (sorry vegans!).

Watch how children enjoy feeding birds in the park. It is the innate nature of our spirit to give love and *seva* keeps this love growing.

Back to Newton's Third Law again – if to every action there is an equal reaction, and assuming that *karma* does exist, then *seva* done with love must give rise to good *karma*. Therefore, when we help others, we shouldn't feel proud, just happy that we have not only helped someone else, we have also helped ourself.

One last thing – if we cannot help, for whatever reason, then we can ensure that we do not harm any living being through thought, word or deed. This is another form of *seva* – doing good through not doing bad.

Some *Seva* Experiences

Establishing a Dental Surgery

On a visit to see Sai Baba in 1997 we were told that we had to set up a dental surgery, and that it would be an instant success. We spent many hours looking at practices that were for sale, but couldn't find one that was suitable. We decided that we must build one up from scratch, as then we could have everything just as we liked.

We found suitable premises, fitted them out as a dental surgery, hired staff, and opened the doors, As Baba had told us, it was successful from the start.

Although we didn't realise it at the time, our surgery provided us with many opportunities for *seva*:

— We would treat ANYBODY. Many people these days find it hard to find an NHS dentist and have difficulty affording private fees. We welcomed everybody, whether they wanted NHS treatment, were exempt from charges or wanted certain treatment done privately.
— We tried always to offer service with a smile and treated patients as if they were guests in our own home, by offering them cups of tea or coffee and a friendly chat whilst they were waiting.
— Wherever possible, the elderly or those who found it very difficult to get to the surgery were offered home visits.
— By the relief of pain and suffering we made our patients' lives a little more comfortable. Most people would not consider dental extractions or fillings to be *seva,* but it is service if the relief of pain is done in a loving way.
— We tried to ensure that our staff had pleasant working conditions, and the money that they earned helped to support them and their families. In addition, the money that we earned improved our standard of living.

Prison Dentristry

'Once I had a dream that I should go and look after prison inmates. When reading my new *British Dental*

82

Journal the next day, I found a position immediately. I phoned up, arranged an interview, and was offered the job! I was the prison dentist one day a week and found that it was a wonderful experience. I worked in a maximum security prison housing serious offenders, but Sai Baba had told me that they were all his "babies" and I should look after them as such. The atmosphere in the Dental Unit was like an ashram and none of the prisoners ever gave me any trouble at all. I was very grateful that I had been given the chance to love and serve a different sort of patient.' D.P.

Feeding the Poor and Hungry

If we always keep our heart and mind open then opportunities for *seva* will present themselves to us. However, they do not always take the form that we most expect.

'After we sold our dental practice, I went to India to spend some time at Sai Baba's ashram, and, hopefully, do some *seva*. I was keeping my options open, but nevertheless, I took my dental certificates and some instruments with me.

'Initially I found no opportunity to do any dentistry, but I did find work serving food to the poor and hungry. Feeding people sounds very easy. It is, and it is also one of the most spiritually rewarding and humbling experiences. I had thought that the only way I could help people was by fixing their teeth and here I was, now helping to fill their stomachs.

'Imagine what opportunities we have, as parents, husbands, wives or partners, to give *seva* through providing good nutritious meals served with love to our nearest and dearest.

'It was whilst serving food to the poor that I was

approached to help with a medical camp where the dentist had been taken ill, so my chance to do dentistry did eventually materialise.' D.P.

An African Medical Camp

'I was recently involved with a medical camp in Zambia. The area chosen was extremely poor; many people there go for days at a time with no food. In that region thirty per cent of individuals are infected with HIV and the average age of mortality is thirty-seven years.

'After months of planning by our UK organisers and their Zambian contacts, a group of doctors, surgeons, opticians, dentists, pharmacists and complementary health practitioners took over a school for two weeks and turned it into a medical centre.

'We were extremely fortunate that everything went according to plan and I believe that this was because everything was done with the right intentions. Our journey went smoothly and we cleared customs without incident, together with tonnes of medical equipment. We had flown a dental chair over with us; miraculously this turned out to be self-contained and so didn't require plumbing in as expected. (This was a good thing, as we had no reliable plumber or electrician.)

'When the patients arrived, we saw so much disease, pain and hunger that it invoked real compassion. I had read about compassion but never felt it like this. Many of us felt very uncomfortable, when we were given food three times a day, knowing that most of our patients, and even our school student helpers, were fortunate if they ate even once a day.

'There were rumours that some of the products that were given to patients, such as spectacles and drugs,

84

were sold outside the camp. I did not see this for myself, and if it did happen it was only a small minority of people who were involved, as is usually the case. Even so, this news caused a lot of resentment amongst some of us, but there was little that we could do. We could not punish all the patients for the actions of just a few. Even if one life had benefited from our work, and as long as actions are done with pure love, that is enough.'

'Whoever saves a single soul saves the world.' MISHNAH SANHEDRIN

'In addition to feeling compassion for the African patients, we all assumed that we were there to help *them*. However, we found that they helped *us*, by giving us so much love in return for both basic advice and complex treatment. This love often brought tears to the eyes of even hardened hospital consultants.

'We also learnt the importance of looking after each other. We were working between twelve and twenty hours a day (it varied between departments). We had to serve each other in order to keep going and some people did get sick on their return to England, as a result of overworking. (Remember *ahimsa* and how overwork is violence?)

'We all learnt that, when involved in a camp, it is very important that we look after ourselves, get adequate rest and drink plenty of fluids, especially in hot climates.

'Before going off on the camp, I questioned myself as to what difference a few days' health care would make to people. I soon realised just how much difference we did actually make to the lives of those we treated. A caring, helpful face and hands, kind words, advice, treatment and the relief of pain – all these give hope, confidence and faith to those in despair and pain.

85

'The patients we treated taught us a lesson by their immense patience. There was never any pushing and shoving as they queued for treatment. Many of them had walked in the heat for up to two days in order to reach us, with no food, little water and often carrying small children, yet they felt that they and the other patients were all in the same boat and so were happy to wait their turn.

'A few local people, who were relatively wealthy in comparison with their fellow compatriots, approached us. They also wanted the advice of Western medical professionals. Some of us were not happy about treating these people, who could afford to pay to see local doctors, but we were there to love all and serve all.

'Why should a rich person be ostracised just because he or she has wealth? We often feel somehow that a person has no excuse not to be well or happy if they are wealthy, yet they need to be served and loved just like everyone else. At this camp, *all* were invited, so we had to treat everyone, no matter how rich or poor.' D.P.

If one is poor, people feel pity, or if one is lucky, compassion. In comparison, if one is wealthy, one is often 'shunned' by society. Many people feel that a rich person is not entitled to love or even a smile, as punishment for having lots of money.

Society accepts a person who is neither too rich nor too poor much more readily. Such a person appears open and available to others who, unsure of exactly how much the individual is worth, do not feel threatened or inferior.

Karma Yoga

'We must always remember that we are little instruments in His hands. The work we do is God's work.

86

The moment we begin to say, "It is I, it is my work", then it becomes selfish.'

Mother Theresa

As discussed earlier in the LOVE chapter, through selfless service we are embarking on what is known in *Vedic* terms as the *karma yoga* pathway to enlightenment.

A *karma yogi* serves others without desire for reward and with no mind on the fruits of the labour. The work is done with unconditional love and so does not lead to grief or disappointment.

When we are constantly mindful of the outcome of our actions, our ego becomes involved and these actions often lead to unhappiness, stress, anxiety and illness. Think of all that individuals such as parents and teachers have done to make us who and what we are. Surely we owe it to them and society to serve or help others in some way?

'*Seva* rendered in the faith that all are forms of the one God is the highest karma. You must watch and see that the inspiration for the *seva* comes from the heart and not the head.' Sai Baba, *Sri Sathya Sai Speaks* Vol. 9 25:136

EPILOGUE

'Human suffering is not a sign of God's anger with mankind. It is a sign, rather, of man's ignorance of the divine law. The law is forever infallible in its workings.'

Sri Kriyananda, The Essence of Self-Realisation.

The human values discussed in the preceding chapters are a way of life rather than a religious doctrine or cult. All the values are inter-related, so they can be taken and practised one by one. When we start to live our life according to just one of the values, we are well on our way to following them all.

No one would disagree that there is great suffering in the world today. If one is poor, one might suffer through physical hardship and want; if one is rich one often suffers mentally, with depression and anxiety.

However, it is also an irrefutable fact that there is great joy to be found in such things as beautiful countryside, good food, a fulfilling job or a loving relationship.

If we introduce the six human values into our lives, then whatever happens to us we will always be blissful and have peace and joy in our hearts.

Peace in the World – It Is Possible

'The works of love are the works of peace. If we try

to love one another the way God loves us, we will have peace.'

Mother Theresa

If we all started to consider the feelings of others for a change, even in the mundane areas of life, by such actions as queuing patiently, letting people off the train before we push our way on or treating shop assistants with respect rather than condescension, then eventually this love and respect for our fellow man would spread through all of society and the whole world would improve. Human suffering, anxiety and fear would all disappear and there would be Peace on Earth.

A Few Words of Caution

As with everything, moderation is the key. Attempting to implement all the human values overnight will lead to disharmony in thought, word and deed. To make a long-term difference in our lives we must understand, visualise and experience the human values rather than just follow them slavishly.

You have to really *believe* in the human values. If you try to suppress certain tendencies on a superficial level, then you will just become ill. The desire for change must come from *deep within you*.

An example of this is vegetarianism. It is relatively simple for anyone apart from the most die-hard carnivore to avoid eating meat for a few days, but then one whiff of a bacon sandwich and it all gets forgotten. If we are giving up meat for the right reason, that is, a strong conviction that no living creature should have to die in order to satisfy our taste buds, then we will always stand by that decision.

Each morning, as you prepare for the day ahead, spend a few peaceful minutes reflecting on the human values and how they can be incorporated into your daily routine. In the evening, as you give thanks for the day, ask yourself whether you have followed the human values to your best ability. Can you learn from anything you experienced today? Can you improve yourself in any way?

Never ever expect to live the human values through your partner. Spiritual growth is not something that can be delegated to your husband or wife as if it were the weekly shop or the housework.

We often look to our partners for the qualities that we ourselves are lacking. This is one reason why some people seem unable to stay with one partner for more than a short time before moving on to the next. Once the 'honeymoon period' is over these people expect their partner to deal with the inadequacies that *they* feel subconsciously and become disillusioned when this doesn't happen.

When we realise that our inadequacies remain, rather than look within, we blame the other person. We feel anger, we feel resentment, and another relationship ends. We must change ourselves before we try to change others.

Act Today!

Many of you who have read this book will be thinking, 'It all sounds like a good idea in theory but I'm too busy/poor/tired/lazy to implement any of these human values in my life. I'm not a bad person really, maybe I can try it when I retire/win the lottery/get a promotion.'

Don't wait until tomorrow, for we all know that tomorrow never comes. WE MUST ALL ACT NOW. Start making changes in your life right away!

Liberation (*Moksha*)

When we are buried deep in our earthly existence (*samsara*) we may occasionally get glimpses of liberation. These are often only transient but we enjoy them a great deal. Think of a pleasant scene on holiday, a walk in the park on a crisp autumn morning or time spent with people we love. We wish that all of life could be like this but feel that this is an impossible dream.

Through constant self-analysis and self-improvement we *can* achieve permanent liberation. As we learn to listen to our inner self *(atma)*, we shed all those preconceptions that hold us back on our spiritual path. Once we realise that we are all divine, we gain freedom from the effects of life's ups and downs and achieve permanent BLISS.

GLOSSARY

AHIMSA – literally non-harm; non-violence, non-injury, gentleness to all.

ANANDA – joy, bliss, happiness.

ASANA – literally a seat or throne (of a deity). A posture that steadies the body and calms the mind.

ASHRAM – literally without conflict, shelter, haven. A guru's establishment where one can seek enlightenment.

ATMA – the eternal spirit, our soul.

AVATAR – literally one who descends; an incarnation of God.

AYURVEDA – literally knowledge of longevity. A traditional Hindu system of medicine.

BHAGAVAD-GITA – 'The Song of God', the name given to the eighteen-chapter section of the epic *Mahabharata*, which contains the dialogue between Krishna and Arjuna. The text teaches the understanding of *dharma* and devotion to God.

BHAKTI YOGA – (*bhaj* – to serve, love, worship). The yogic path of devotion that leads to union with God and involves such practices as chanting and prayer.

CHAKRA – literally wheel. The *chakras* are seven potential energy centres located in the astral body from the crown of the head to the base of the spine.

CHIT – consciousness, awareness, knowledge.

DARSHAN – to see a great person and receive his or her blessing. Sathya Sai Baba's twice daily public appearances are called *darshans*.

92

DHARMA – duty, righteousness, a set of principles for a righteous life

EGO – the 'I' or self; that part of us that is conscious and thinks; an image of oneself.

GURU – spiritual master.

HATHA YOGA – the physical branch of the meditative *raja yoga*. *Hatha yoga* uses *asanas* (postures) to achieve physical relaxation and awaken the spiritual centres of the body.

JNANA YOGA – (*jna* – to know). Union with God via the intellectual/philosophical yogic pathway. This usually involves the study of the *Vedanta* philosophy of the *Upanishads*.

KARMA – literally deed, action; the law of cause and effect; those actions or consequences that must be borne as a result of other actions (good and bad) done in the past, especially in previous incarnations.

KARMA YOGA – (*kri* – to do, act). Union with God through selfless service.

LIBERATION – see *moksha*, self-realisation.

MAHABHARATA – an ancient Sanskrit Indian epic containing the *Bhagavad-Gita*.

MAYA – illusion. The whole world is *maya*, a divine illusion. The only reality is God.

MEDITATION – the attainment of supreme spiritual peace through mental stillness and inner calm.

MOKSHA – self-realisation; liberation from an earthly existence (*samsara*).

NIRVANA – bliss; union with God.

PRANA – Life-force, vital energy.

PRASHANTI NILAYAM – Sathya Sai Baba's ashram in Puttaparthi, Andra Pradesh, India.

PREMA – love.

RAJA YOGA – (*raja* – royal). Union with God through

control of the mind. A scientific approach also referred to as *ashtanga yoga*.

REINCARNATION – to be born again in another body or form. Hindus believe that we were originally all part of God but have forgotten our true nature and until we become self-realised we will be trapped in an endless cycle of birth and death.

SAMADHI – literally original balance; state of union with God; very deep meditation, super-conscious state or trance in which one loses the ego identity and experiences bliss.

SAMSARA – the cycle of worldly existence; worldly life.

SATCHITANANDA – literally truth-consciousness-bliss. The supreme state.

SATHYA – truth, true.

SELF-REALISATION – see *moksha* and liberation. The knowledge that God is omnipresent; realisation that we are all Divine and embodiments of God.

SEVA – selfless service.

SHANTI – peace.

SWAMI – literally master, teacher. Form of address for a guru.

UPANISHADS – literally sitting down near; i.e. the pupil sitting down in front of the master. Ancient Sanskrit scriptures containing the *Vedas*, central tenets of the *Vedanta* philosophy.

VIBUTI – literally manifestation, wonderful, marvellous; sacred ash such as that manifested by Sathya Sai Baba.

VEDAS – literally knowledge; the earliest Hindu and Indo-European scriptures of which the *Upanishads* are the concluding parts.

VEDANTA – literally the end of the *Vedas*. One of the six major schools of Hindu philosophy, based on a close examination of the *Upanishads*.

YOGA – literally yoking, union. Union of the individual soul with the Universal Soul i.e. God; the various methods and practices adopted to achieve this.

YOGI – spiritual aspirant seeking union with God by means of various mental practices; one who has achieved this goal.

BIBLIOGRAPHY

Balu, Shakuntala, *Living Saint* (Describes the life and work of Mother Theresa). Sawbridge Enterprises Ltd, London, 1985

Breuilly, Elizabeth and Palmer, Martin, *Religions of the World*. Harper Collins Publishers Ltd, London, 1999

Easwaran, Eknath, *Gandhi the Man*. Jaico Publishing House, Mumbai, 1998

Gandhi, Mohandas K., *The Way to God*. Berkeley Hills Books, Berkeley, California, 1999

Judith, Anodea, *The Truth About Chakras*. Llewellyn Publications, St. Paul, Minnesota, 1994

New Testament, Gideons New International Version

Organic magazine, published bimonthly by wViP, a division of Highbury House Communications PLC, London

Ruhela, S.P., *The Sai Trinity*. Vikas Publishing House PVT Ltd, New Delhi, 1997

Steel, Brian, *The Sathya Sai Baba Compendium*. Samuel Weiser, Inc. Maine, 1997

Sturgess, Steven, *The Yoga Book, A Practical Guide to Self-Realisation*. Element Books, Shaftesbury, Dorset, 1997

Sathya Sai Baba, *Sathya Sai Speaks, Volumes I–XV*. Sathya Sai Books and Publications Trust, Prashanti Nilayam, India

Sivananda Yoga Vedanta Centre, *Yoga Mind and Body*. Dorling Kindersley, London, 1998

The Big Issue magazine, published weekly by The Big Issue, London

The Vegan magazine, published quarterly by The Vegan Society, St. Leonards-on-Sea, East Sussex

The Vegetarian magazine, published quarterly by The Vegetarian Society, Altrincham, Cheshire

Peta's Animal Times magazine, published quarterly by People for the Ethical Treatment of Animals, London